VALERIE DREGO

END ZONE

Prophetic Timelines and the Last Days

Copyright © 2017 Valerie Drego. All Rights Reserved.

No part of this book may be reproduced in whole or in part, in any form, or stored on any device including digital media, except with the prior written permission of the author and/or publisher. Exceptions are granted for brief quotations utilized in critical articles or reviews with due credit given to the author. The contents of this book are the result of extensive research by the author and every effort has been made to ensure that the information in this book was correct at press time. However the author and publisher do not assume and hereby disclaim any liability to any party for any loss, disruption or damage caused by errors or omissions, whether such error or omissions result from negligence, accident, or any other cause. The author and publisher disclaim any liability in connection with the use of the information in this book. All scripture quoted is from the Holy Bible, King James Version.

Library and Archives Canada Cataloguing in Publication

Drego, Valerie, author
    End zone--prophetic timelines and the last days / Valerie Drego.

ISBN 978-1-926926-82-7 (softcover)

    1. Bible--Prophecies--End of the world. 2. End of the world--Biblical teaching. I. Title.

BS649.E63D74 2017   236›.9   C2017-902454-X

Published by:
In Our Words Inc. /inourwords.ca / inourwords@bell.net
251 Queen Street South, Suite #561, Streetsville, ON L5M 1L7

Cover image: Shutterstock

Cover design: Victoria Drego

this book is dedicated to
Gladys Lilian Vas de Sousa
and Dr. Eustace Xavier de Sousa

to mum and dad with love, always

Rejoice in the LORD, O ye righteous:
for praise is comely for the upright
…
By the word of the LORD were the heavens made;
and all the host of them by the breath of his mouth
…
For he spake and it was done;
he commanded and it stood fast.
The LORD bringeth the counsel of the heathen
to naught: he maketh the devices of the people
of none effect
…
Behold, the eye of the LORD is upon them that
fear him, upon them that hope in his mercy:
To deliver their soul from death,
and to keep them alive in famine.
Our soul waiteth for the LORD:
he is our help and our shield
…
Let thy mercy, O LORD, be upon us,
according as we hope in thee.

[Psalm 33:1, 6, 9-10, 18-20, 22]

Acknowledgements

I would like to acknowledge those men and women – scientists, authors, Bible students and prophecy scholars, both in current time and in the past – whose contributions are duly credited within this book. Their solid scholarship and sometimes visionary work brought me growth and sparked personal insight, part of which is recorded here.

I would like to thank my family, most especially my husband Don, for their love, support and patience through countless hours of study, online research, books, lectures and podcasts that went into the writing of this book.

I would like to thank Amanda D. for her work on the graphics; Victoria D. for cover effects; and Shirley A. for in-text design.

And I would like to thank my editor and publisher Cheryl Antao-Xavier who helped this book happen.

All scripture quoted is from the Holy Bible, King James Version.

May His harvest be increased.

Table of Contents

Dedication

Psalm 33, excerpts

Acknowledgements

Chapter 1 – the Bible as Math, 9

Chapter 2 – the Feasts of Our Lord, 27

Chapter 3 – Names, 51

Chapter 4 – Daniel, the visions, 75

Chapter 5 – the Seventy-Weeks Prophecy, 111

Chapter 6 – the Book of Revelation, 143

Chapter 7 – the Challenge of Free Will and an Age of Deceit, 179

Chapter 8 – Isaiah, the pyramid text, 225

Chapter 9 – 2017, a marker, 245

About the Author

1 – the Bible as Math

The Bible is the holy and inspired word of God.

The sixty-six books of the Old and New Testament were written over a period of one thousand five hundred years by forty authors of varied background; yet the Bible never contradicts itself. It stands not as an anthology but a unified whole. Its key tenets remain unchanged. It is validated by the ancient law of witness, confirmed by two or more re-affirmations across this stretch of time, *that in the mouth of two or three witnesses every word may be established,* (Matt.18:16; Deut.17:6; 2 Cor.13:1).

The Bible reaches back to tell the story of creation.

It declares world history before it unfolds.

It foretells the end.

It proclaims God as Creator and Redeemer, the first and the last, the beginning and the end, by whose breath all life exists.

The Bible demands faith but it offers a crutch to those who falter.

That crutch is math.

Math is structured around quantity, space and form. It is predicated upon constants. The principles that govern math are not bound by culture or region but speak in a universal language of numbers, symbols and ciphers which do not alter over time. And math has one further advantage: it has grades of relevancy, adjusted to the capacity of the student.

Thus in kindergarten we learn that one plus one is two, and we are proud of that knowledge; in primary school we advance to levels of greater addition and subtraction; in middle school we learn multiplication and division and the rudiments of algebra; the high school student will learn abstract equations, geometry and the value of *pi* and (maybe) trigonometry and triangular numbers; the student of advanced math will study calculus and fractals, the existence of theoretical numbers and the Mandelbrot Set, and the value of *e* which is the base of natural logarithm and the exponential function of infinity, a concept employed in wave mechanics, electrical theory and the distribution of prime.

Question: what has this to do with the Bible?

Let us start with the first verse of Genesis –

In the beginning God created the heaven and the earth, (Gen.1:1).

This well-known creation verse of the Old Testament finds its counterpart in the equally well-known opening of the gospel of John –

In the beginning was the Word, and the Word was with God, and the Word was God, (John 1:1).

These verses from Genesis and John are the two most-quoted creation verses of the Bible; and in creation there are only two dimensionless constants: *pi* which is the ratio of a circle's circumference to its diameter (valued at 3.14159265… ∞) and *e* which is the base of natural logarithm (valued at 2.71828182… ∞), whose function is used in exponential growth and decay, forming the limit of $(1+\frac{1}{n})^n$, as n approaches infinity.

So again, what is the connection?

Hebrew, the original script of the Old Testament, and Greek, the original script of the New Testament, possess a unique property: they are alphanumeric. Neither language has a separate set of characters to represent numbers (1, 2, 3…), instead every letter of the alphabet carries a numeric value. The first letter of the alphabet has a value of one, the second letter a value of two, the eleventh letter is valued at twenty, and so on. Each word and each sentence can therefore be assigned a value.

Thus, in Hebrew, *In the beginning God created the heaven and the earth* (Gen.1:1, figure i) has a numeric value of 2701. In a brilliant online study, John Nuyten (seminar, *The Living Word: God's Grand Design*) identifies 2701 as the 73rd triangular number, and the product of two prime numbers 37, 73 (note the mirror image). Dr. Charles Missler (essay, *Fundamental Constants,* 2003, citing the work of Dr. Peter Bluer) adds an amazing dimension to this verse.

If we take:

$$\frac{[\text{no. of letters}] \times [\text{product of letters}]}{[\text{no. of words}] \times [\text{product of words}]}$$

$$= 3.1416 \times 10^{17}$$

$$= pi \times 10^{17}$$

pi, the first dimensionless constant of the universe, appears.

And, in Greek, *In the beginning was the Word, and the Word was with God, and the Word was God* (John 1:1, figure ii) has a value of 3627. The number 3627

English translation (King James Version):
Genesis 1:1, In the beginning God created the heaven and the earth.

Hebrew original (script right to left):

| 296 | 407 | 395 | 401 | 86 | 203 | 913 |

בראשית ברא אלוהים את השמים ואת הארץ

Hebrew alphabet with numerical values:

20	10	9	8	7	6	5	4	3	2	1
י	כ	ט	ח	ז	ו	ה	ד	ג	ב	א

400	300	200	100	90	80	70	60	50	40	30
צ	ק	ר	ש	ת	פ	ע	ס	נ	מ	ל

Fig. i: Hebrew alphabet; Genesis 1:1 with values

is the product of 39, 93 (once again a mirror image), which may also be written as the product of the prime numbers 13, 3, 3, 31 (again mirrored); 3627 is not a triangular number, but when added to 2701 it gives the 112th triangular number, 6328, as though informing the

---

English translation (King James Version) John 1:1

In the beginning was the Word,

and the Word was with God,

and the Word was God.

Greek original with numerical values:

55   719   58   70   373
ΕΝ ΑΡΧΗΙ ΗΝ Ο ΛΟΓΟΣ

31   70   373   58   450   420   134
ΚΑΙ Ο ΛΟΓΟΣ ΗΝ ΠΡΟΣ ΤΟΝ ΘΕΟΝ

31   284   58   70   373
ΚΑΙ ΘΕΟΣ ΗΝ Ο ΛΟΓΟΣ

Greek alphabet with numerical values:

1	2	3	4	5	6	7	8	9	10	20	30	40
Α	Β	Γ	Δ	Ε	F	Ζ	Η	Θ	Ι	Κ	Λ	Μ

50	60	70	80	90	100	200	300	400	500	600	700	800
Ν	Ξ	Ο	Π	Ϙ	Ρ	Σ	Τ	Υ	Φ	Χ	Ψ	Ω

Fig. ii: The Greek alphabet; John 1:1 with values

reader that the New Testament is locked onto the Old Testament by God's design. The verse has one further dimension.

If we take:

$$\frac{[\text{no. of letters}] \times [\text{product of letters}]}{[\text{no. of words}] \times [\text{product of words}]}$$
$$= 2.7183 \times 10^{65}$$
$$= e \times 10^{65}$$

e, the second dimensionless constant of the universe, appears.

pi and *e* are transcendental numbers. This means that neither number is the root of any algebraic equation with integer coefficients.

A radical agnostic might argue that a mathematician meddled with the first verse in Genesis (just for a laugh); then, several centuries later – a thousand plus years, in fact – another math whizz inserted an abstruse equation into the gospel of John (do mathematicians have an odd sense of humour?) – but at this point we leave humour and run up against fact. Although the knowledge of *pi* existed in imprecise form as early as Babylonian times, the principle of *e* was only discovered by the Scottish mathematician Sir John Napier in 1614; it was fully explored seventy years later by the Swiss mathematicians Jacob Bernoulli and Leonhard Euler. Euler calculated the value of *e* to 23 decimal places and Euler's choice of the symbol *e* is said to have been retained in his honour.

Astounded? There is more.

When examined in its original Hebrew and Greek, the Bible is filled with numeric patterns. These math patterns appear to be the seal of God, a watermark of authenticity. Unbelievers, gathering to deride, have not been able to explain their overwhelming and multilayered presence in the Bible.

In fact, Bible numerics were first identified by the Russian scientist, nihilist and agnostic Dr. Ivan Panin, in the late nineteenth century. His conversion, in 1890, made headlines around the world. Learning Hebrew and Greek, and working by hand without any form of mechanical aid, Panin studied the number seven, and multiples thereof, as one of the most prolific numeric series in scripture.

What does this mean?

Let us use Genesis 1:1 again –

In the beginning God created the heaven and the earth

In Hebrew, this opening verse of the Bible is composed of 7 words(i) and 28 ($7x4$) letters(ii); the three nouns(iii) *God, heaven, earth* total 14 letters ($7x2$) with a numeric value(iv) of 777 ($7x111$); the single verb(v) *created* has a value of 203 ($7x29$) – it provides an interlocking rhythm of sevens embedded in a single sentence. Patterns of seven, both overt and structural (consonant and vowel, verb and noun, tense, vocabulary and gender), cover every page of the

Bible. The genealogy of Christ in the first chapter of Matthew delivers an incredible, entwined pattern of over 34 classes of heptads locking together within the rigid grammar of Greek to announce his line of ancestry. The possibility of random chance for their unified, interlinked presence exceeds the statistical impossibility of one in a trillion.

Panin spent the next fifty years of his life scrutinising scripture, in excess of three million words (or over twenty million characters), digging up what he identified as the heptadic structure of the text, generating 43,000 pages of patterns that link across the sixty-six books of the Bible proving some great overseeing authority.

Part of his amazing work is accessible online.

We are, of course, familiar with the obvious sevens of the Bible. The seven days of creation in Genesis, the seven pairs of 'clean' animals in the flood story, the seven feasts of God, the seven-day circling of Jericho, and the multiple sevens of Revelation – the seven candlesticks, the seven churches, the seven seals, the seven trumpets, the seven thunders, the seven bowls of judgement. We have Christ's admonition to forgive *not seven times, but until seventy times seven* (Matt.18:22). We have the seven sentences Jesus spoke from the cross (Luke 23:34, 43, 46; John 19:26-27, 28, 30; Matt.27:46 echoed in Mark 15:34). And we know that *our years are three-score years and ten* (Psalm 90:10), the persistent seven appearing again.

Let us briefly step from the word of God to his creation, man. Did you know that the human pulse beats slower every seventh day? This medical mystery, first identified in the twentieth century, has no scientific explanation. It is sometimes called the biological Shabbat clock since it mimics the seventh day of rest ordained by God.

The resting heart averages seventy beats a minute.

Every cell in the human body is renewed every seven years.

Seven is a mystical number tied to the completion of God's work. Time itself is carved into huge swaths of seven. We have the six thousand years allotted to man in Genesis 6:3 (explained later) and the millennial kingdom of Revelation 20:4, giving a total span of seven thousand years. Within this broad sweep of time appear sub-blocks of time, also in sevens, tracking between major biblical events.

One such study is the example below. Of special interest in this presentation is the number 296, the numeric value of *earth*:

| From the creation of Adam to Abraham's sacrifice | ... | 2072yrs (7x296) |
| From Abraham's sacrifice to Christ | ... | 2072yrs (7x296) |

Within these major time blocks appear smaller sets of seven, as illustrated below. An attempt has been made in this study to tie biblical data to secular dates (some events overlap):

>From Jericho (Nigro/Marchetti dig)
to Judges (Garstang dig) ...   490yrs (7x70)
From David (temple planned)
to Cyrus (temple decreed) ...   490yrs (7x70)
From Solomon (temple built)
to Darius (temple rebuilt) ...   490yrs (7x70)

Nestling within these subsets are other blocks of seven, both mundane and prophetic: the seven-year agricultural cycle prescribed by the Torah; Jacob's seven years of plenty and seven years of famine; the seventy years of Babylonian captivity prophesized by Jeremiah; and the immensely prophetic Seventy Weeks of Daniel, playing out today.

Numerics are not confined to seven though the heptadic structure is the most abundant. Other sets of numbers appear, woven loosely, interspersed, like a riff of music or a chord.

The number forty appears, associated with waiting or testing, as in the forty days spent by Moses on Mount Sinai, (Exo.34:28); forty years of wandering in the wilderness, (Deut.2:7); a forty-day taunting of the Israelites by Goliath, (1Sam.17:6); Christ's forty-day fast in the Judean Desert, (Luke 4:2).

The notion of jubilee appears (Lev.25:10), a fiftieth year following seven sevens, to be celebrated as a year of release and return.

The one-hundred-and-twenty-year time-cycle appears, *And the LORD said, My spirit shall not always strive with man, for that he also is flesh: yet his days shall be an hundred and twenty years,* (Gen.6:3).

Interlocking patterns of three also surface.

Scholars, following in Panin's footsteps, have unearthed multiple numeric patterns woven into the fabric of the text, too numerous to list here, too consistent to be deemed accidental. These patterns do not merely cover the surface of the text but sink deep into it like roots into soil, a discovery made by accident.

During World War I, Michael Weissmandl, a Czechoslovakian mathematician and rabbi, chanced upon an obscure reference in the fourteenth century work of Rabbeynu Bachayah, referencing a pattern of letters encoded in the Torah. It inspired Weissmandl to further study and he encouraged his students likewise. In the mid-1980s, the Israeli mathematicians Witztum, Rips and Rosenberg designed a software program which permitted an equidistant letter sequence to be carried out in analysing the Masoretic Text of the Old Testament (ELS, i.e. skipping a fixed, predetermined number of letters to the next letter). Their breakthrough work is discussed in Michael Drosnin's, *The Bible Code*.

Using ELS, the word T-O-R-H (Torah, Hebrew name for the first five books of the Bible) appears in Genesis and Exodus at a skip of fifty; H-R-O-T appears in Numbers and Deuteronomy, also at a skip of fifty, spelling Torah backwards. The four books seem to point to the middle book, the book of laws. In Leviticus, at a skip of seven, appears the holy name of God, Y-H-W-H.

The math of ELS affirms an omniscient authority as the source of the Bible, one not limited by our space-time continuum. Encoded in the original text is information on events occurring centuries into the future, even into our time – while simultaneously preventing prophetic utterance; that is, the encoded information about a future event cannot be pulled out of the text in advance of the event. Grabbing at words or a name (which has been done) most often leads to false prediction; but post facto, with complete and full knowledge, the event is found revealed with odd, specific detail: as, for example, the Lincoln and Kennedy assassinations with all associated names, the place and the year; so too the French Revolution, the Great Depression, the Brexit vote.

Some mathematicians have refused the biblical claim, declaring that any sufficiently large text will render some readable word.

True, perhaps.

And some readable word is exactly right.

No other text offers the abundance, consistency and meaningfulness found in the Bible; no other book holds prophecy within the code.

Astonishingly, every messianic passage in the Old Testament carries the name 'Jesus' within it, in varying skip sequences. Genesis declares, using a skip of 521 letters, 'Yeshua yakhol' which translates 'Jesus is able.'

The explosive power of ELS may be seen in numerous published studies on the subject. We will look at two examples here, drawn from the work of Yacov Rambsel, (his book, *His Name Is Jesus*).

The first is from Isaiah 53:7-10, a powerful text which foretells the suffering and death of Christ in prophetic detail. Beginning with the phrase, *He shall prolong his days…*, Rambsel counted forward every twentieth Hebrew letter to form the phrase 'Yeshua shmi' which translated means, 'Jesus is my name.' Crisscrossing this short chapter in ELS are the words Messiah, Nazarene, Galilee, Passover, Herod, Caesar, Annas High Priest, Caiaphas High Priest, Mary, Kefa (Cephas/Peter), Jochanan (John), Thoma (Thomas), Yakov (James), Shimeon (Simon), Tadira (Thaddaeus), Mataeus (Matthias), bread, wine, his disciples, his cross, let him be crucified.

The second example is from Exodus 30:13-20. Here we find the names of Jesus and Mary (Mary appears thrice, for the three women of that name associated with the crucifixion, cited in Mark 15:40 -

Mary, the mother of Jesus; Mary, the mother of James; and Mary Magdalene), each disciple is mentioned by name, the words Messiah, Nazarene, Passover and Galilee appear, and once again that horrible phrase 'let him be crucified.' Significantly, the words crisscross a text which deals with atonement, *And thou shalt take the atonement money of the children of Israel… before the LORD, to make an atonement for your souls,* (Exo.30:16).

The code beneath the surface text has been lying there, hidden, for approximately three thousand five hundred years.

Equidistant sequencing and the heptadic structure of the Bible are, separately and jointly, an incredible validation of the Bible as deliberate design, a definitive demonstration of the inspired word of God reserved for an age of technological advancement that is drifting into disbelief.

Is more proof needed?

Probably not, but there is more.

The name Jesus carries the Greek numeric value 888; a number that is doubled or tripled emphasises the quality of that number; in the Bible, 8 signifies resurrection. Dr. John Henry (his essay, *Jesus = 888*), arrives at this same value for the descriptive phrases the Lion of Judah, Finished Cross, Divine Presence, Coming Truth, Law of Liberty, Spirit Birth.

The name *Christ* carries the numeric value 1480.

$$\frac{1480}{888} = 1.6666....$$

Strangely enough, or not strangely at all, this is the exact value of the Mercy Seat described in Exodus. The dimensions are precise, *And thou shalt make a mercy seat of pure gold: two cubits and a half shall be the length thereof, and a cubit and a half the breadth thereof,* (Exo.25:17).

$$\frac{2.5}{1.5} = \frac{5}{3} = 1.6666....$$

Jesus Christ is our Mercy Seat.
One more message appears in this lode of gold:

$$\frac{1480}{5} = 296$$

$$\frac{888}{3} = 296$$

296 is the numeric value of *earth*.

The math of Jesus Christ reaffirms a message of mercy to his creation.

In fact the 5:3 ratio, also known as the golden ratio, belongs within the math series called the Fibonacci sequence, named after the Italian mathematician who identified it in the twelfth century, Leonardo Fibonacci. In this math progression, each subsequent number is formed by adding the previous two (thus 1,1,2,3,5,8,13…; figure iii).

Tracing an arc through the diagonal of a golden

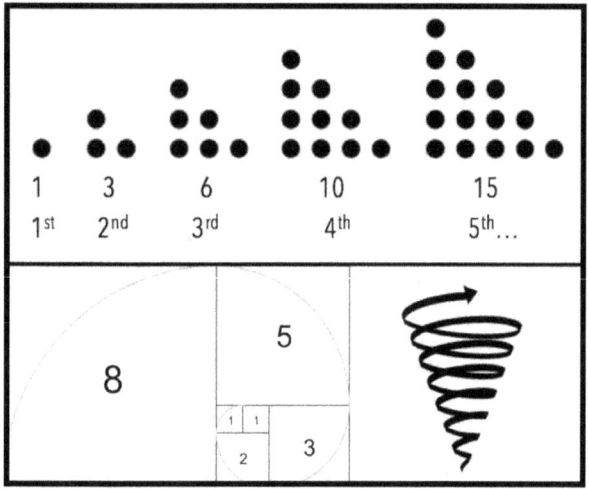

Fig. iii: Triangular Numbers: Fibonacci Sequence and the Golden Spiral

rectangle and carrying it to the next in sequence forms a widening spiral, a spiral we can see everywhere in nature: in the seed distribution of a raspberry, in the display of the florets of a sunflower or the scales of a pinecone, in the delicate spiral of a nautilus shell, in the curve of a wave as it rushes to the shore – the curve, mathematically recorded and plotted onto a graph, reveals the exact points of the Fibonacci sequence. Some call it the fingerprint of God; for as an architect will stamp his work with some distinctive flourish, so has God marked his creation with math.

Obvious math and hidden math.

Math cloaked with beauty, waiting to be found.

Haim Shore, professor of Engineering Sciences,

Ben-Gurion University, Israel, (please google), has used the numeric values of the Hebrew words for *earth, sun* and *moon* to find the size and mass of these objects hidden in their names; amazingly, *or–light* and *kol–sound* hold within themselves the speed of light and sound; colours hold information on their wave length; *gold* and *silver* reveal scientific data on their atomic weight.

A final testament, this one from author and researcher David Flynn, (his book, *Temple at the Center of Time*). Remember *pi*? The little town of Bethlehem lies on latitude 31.70 N, which may also be read as DMS latitude 31° 41' 59" N. These digits form the number sequence of *pi*. A measuring rod extended from the Temple Mount in Jerusalem, to Bethlehem, gives a length of 29,808 feet. This is the exact value of pi^9 (*pi* precisely calculated to five decimal points as it appears in the DMS reading; 9, the biblical number of finality and judgement, the perfect movement of God). This measuring line touches a point on *pi* latitude, a few hundred yards from the Church of the Nativity. It marks a spot outside the old city walls, a fitting place for a stable.

Mind blowing.

And unbelievably true.

2 – the Feasts of Our Lord

What is prophecy? Understood in its strictest sense, prophecy is the declaration of future events that lie beyond natural intelligence to know.

To the prosaic mind, prophecy is confined to stated prediction; but a broader view includes the nuanced, the unstated – types and shadows, patterns and prototypes, what is sometimes called Hebrew parallelism. The parables of Jesus Christ are a form of representative parallelism in story, to aid understanding; prophetic parallelism plays out in reality, in an actual sequence of events which foreshadow a future event, enunciating a theme and foretelling a result. The theme and result stay unchanged but the actual 'true' event that is foretold may play out very differently from its shadow.

All dual chronology prophecy is parallelism.

Some parallelism is in-your-face obvious: as for example the demand made of Abraham for his one remaining son; Isaac carries the wood for his sacrifice up Mount Moriah (Gen.22:6, a sacrifice halted); so too the redemptive plan demands the only son of God as sacrifice; Christ carries his own wood up Mount Calvary (John 19:17, a sacrifice fulfilled); Abraham's obedience wins him a nation; Christ's obedience wins him a people and an everlasting kingdom.

Some parallelism needs to be shown to us: as the brass serpent is lifted up in the wilderness, so will Christ be lifted on the cross, the explicit parallel to this event being drawn by Christ himself, (John 3:14; Num.21:9); a teaching on the temporal and the eternal.

Some parallelism we eventually dig out.

One of the deepest prophecies delivered through parallelism occurs in Leviticus, the third book of the Bible. It is the book of Laws. It draws its name from Levitikon i.e. 'things pertaining to the Levites,' the priestly class of the Israelites. It instructs on the nature of sin offerings and ritual sacrifice, on legal and ethical practices, on purification rites, on the conduct required within the camp, around the holy tabernacle and in the presence of the Lord.

Amid an abundance of minutiae appear the seven feasts commanded by YHWH –

And the LORD spake unto Moses saying, Speak unto the children of Israel and say unto them, Concerning the feasts of the LORD, which ye shall proclaim to be holy convocations, even these are my feasts, (Lev.23:1-2).

The Hebrew word for 'convocation' is 'miqra'

(James Strong, *Strong's Exhaustive Concordance of the Bible*, hereafter referred to as *Strong's Concordance*, no.4744); it carries the primary meaning of meeting but a secondary meaning of rehearsal, as in a meeting to rehearse. The Feasts of Our Lord, announced as 'holy convocations,' may thus be seen as practice sessions, rehearsals anticipating some holy event in the future.

The feasts are:

1. Passover – Nisan 14
2. Unleavened Bread – Nisan 15
3. First Fruits – Nisan 16 (16-22)
4. Pentecost – Sivan 6
5. Trumpets – Tishri 1-2
6. Atonement – Tishri 10
7. Tabernacles – Tishri 15-22

God's calendar is a lunar one. The Biblical year comprises 360 days divided into twelve months, with intercalary days inserted periodically, adjusted within a cycle of thirty lunar years (to pull the months back into line with the seasons). Hence the feasts listed above cannot be matched to fixed days on the Gregorian calendar. Worth noting here, the Jews have two calendars – a religious calendar and civil one (as a business will observe the Gregorian year and also a fiscal year, which might differ).

Nisan is the first month of the religious calendar,

roughly mid-March to mid-April.

Passover, the first feast, is observed on the first full moon of spring.

The Israelites rigidly observed the requirements of each feast without understanding their significance beyond the reason for the first. This was apparent to them: it was in memory of their escape from Egypt, when the angel of death spared those houses marked by the blood of a slaughtered lamb; the other first-born in the land of Egypt died but the Israelites were passed over. It was the final plague which compelled Pharaoh to release them from bondage.

In accordance with the requirement of this feast, the Israelites took a one-year-old male lamb or goat, without blemish, on the tenth day of Nisan. It was slaughtered four days later, on Passover day. In addition to the household sacrifices, the people as a whole presented a lamb to the high priest for slaughter. This sacrificial lamb was tied to the temple altar at the third hour and ceremonially slaughtered on the ninth hour. The high priest would intone the final words of this ritual, It is finished.

[N.B. The Biblical day lasted from sunset to sunset and the hours were typically counted in blocks of three. Thus the first hour (of the daylight section) was 6 a.m.; the third hour, 9 a.m.; the sixth hour, noon; the ninth hour, 3 p.m. The same grouping applied to the night watch.]

For one thousand five hundred years the Israelites faithfully carried out this ritual.

But it was only a holy rehearsal.

It foreshadowed what was to come.

On Nisan 14, the Thursday/Friday of the Hebrew year 3793, which is April 3, 33 A.D., our saviour Jesus Christ was put to death on the cross. He was the lamb without blemish who was led to the slaughter; he hung on the cross for the same six-hour period that the lamb lay on the sacrificial altar; he was the high priest who at the ninth hour declared, It is finished.

These exact words appear in John's gospel –

When Jesus therefore had received the vinegar, he said, It is finished; and he bowed his head, and gave up the ghost, (John 19:30).

The three synoptic gospels provide the balance part of this equation, the hours. The crucifixion and death of Jesus Christ is the only event in the Bible which is precisely tied in its recount with the hours of its occurrence.

Thus, in Mark, *And it was the third hour and they crucified him… And when the sixth hour was come, there was darkness over the whole land until the ninth hour. And at the ninth hour Jesus cried with a loud voice,* (Mark 15:25-34).

In Luke, *And it was about the sixth hour, and there was a darkness over all the earth until the ninth hour. And the sun was darkened and the veil of the temple was rent in the midst,* (Luke 23:44-45).

In Matthew, *Now from the sixth hour there was darkness over all the land unto the ninth hour. And about the ninth hour Jesus cried with a loud voice…And behold, the veil of the temple was rent in twain from the top to the bottom: and the earth did quake, and the rocks rent; And the graves were opened,* (Matt. 27:45-46; 51-52).

Attempts to determine the exact year of Christ's death are complicated by a dearth of definitive information, and confused by multiple dating systems in the history of that time; but it is this three-hour period of darkness, and the earthquake which accompanied it, which permit a secular placing for the crucifixion of Jesus Christ.

The Greek historian Phlegon records, 'Now, in the fourth year of the two hundred and second Olympiad, a great eclipse of the sun occurred at the sixth hour that excelled every other before it, turning the day into such darkness of night that the stars could be seen in heaven, and the earth moved in Bithynia, toppling many buildings in the city of Nicaea.'

[N.B. The first Olympiad took place in 776 B.C., the fourth year of the 202nd Olympiad is 33 A.D.; Bithynia was an ancient kingdom in north-west Asia Minor, modern Turkey.]

The darkness and earthquake is recorded by Thallus, first century, third book of Histories.

Eusebius of Caesarea, an early historian, also

recorded the darkness and earthquake in great detail; his original work is lost but verbatim excerpts appear in the still extant papers of Sextus Julius Africanus [c.160-240 A.D., *Chronographiai*]; and George the Syncellus, ninth century Byzantine historian and monk [d.811 A.D., *Exloge Chronographias,* Chpt.391].

The Acts of Pilate, First Greek Forum, chronicle a letter from Pontius Pilate to the Emperor Tiberius describing the crucifixion darkness (the Bible student will remember that, on account of his wife's dream, Pilate was anxious to free Jesus, finally – literally – washing his hands off the crime, Matt.27:24). Pilate writes, 'At the time he was crucified there was darkness over all the world, the sun being darkened at mid-day, and the stars appearing, but in them was no luster; and the moon, as if turned into blood, failed in her light. And the world was swallowed up by the lower regions, so that the very sanctuary of the temple, as they call it, could not be seen...' [Pilate, personal letter to Tiberius Caesar, compilation, *The Acts of Pilate, First Greek Forum*].

Indeed, NASA can confirm that there was a blood moon on the April 3, 33 A.D., visible in the Holy Land. But the darkness was not a solar eclipse. A solar eclipse can only take place at the new moon, when sun, moon and earth are aligned in syzygy, and the maximum duration of a full solar eclipse cannot exceed 7 minutes, 36 seconds.

The Passover is celebrated at full moon.

A full moon makes any solar eclipse impossible.

We are left with a strange conclusion: the incident was beyond nature, supernatural.

In fact this was the conclusion of Chinese astronomers who also recorded this abnormal darkness in the historic annals of China. In the 30s grouping of the first century (a closer date is not possible, Chinese chronology recorded events on a 60-year cycle), the extended period of darkness is identified as happening, *In the seventh year of Quang-vou-ti, on the day Quei-hay, the last of the Third Moon*; they declared to the Emperor that the inexplicable darkness, not an eclipse, was supernatural and could only signify the death of a God.

There is additional validation for the year 33 A.D. It is the only year between 27-34 A.D., contending years for the crucifixion proposed by Bible scholars, in which Passover preparation falls on Thursday-Friday, and the resurrection on Sunday, as taught by the early church.

Tracking back from this crucifixion date places Christ's birth in 2 B.C.

Does any information support this derived date?

Herod is a significant historical figure, tied to Jesus through the wise men and the slaughter of the Innocents. The Jewish historian Flavius Josephus writes, '[Herod] died having reigned thirty-four years since he had caused Antigonus to be slain, and obtained his kingdom; but thirty-seven years since he had been made king by the Romans,' [Josephus, *War* 1.665(I.33.8)]. Scholars agree that Josephus recorded events by the Jewish calendar but some believe it was the religious calendar and others the civil; if a reign started at the end of a year, then the 'first year' was sometimes thirteen or fourteen months long; again, did Herod complete his thirty-seventh year of kingship or did he die during the thirty-seventh year?

With these constraints, we may conclude that Herod's thirty-seventh year lies between 4 B.C. and 2 B.C., with his death a year later.

Prior to the twentieth century, any post 4 B.C. suggestion for the birth of Jesus Christ was immediately discounted because Josephus also placed Herod's death close to a lunar eclipse, and a full lunar eclipse appears in Jewish annals, recorded in 4 B.C. However, technological advancements have allowed NASA to confirm two lunar eclipses in 1 B.C.: a total lunar eclipse January 10, 1 B.C.; a partial lunar eclipse December 29, 1 B.C.

Is there separate substantiating data for a 2 B.C. birth?

Actually, yes. A dance of the stars.

And God said, let there be lights in the firmament of the heaven to divide the day from the night; and let them be for signs, and for seasons, and for days, and years, (Gen.1:14).

The Hebrew word for 'sign' is 'moed', more accurately translated as appointment (*Strong's Concordance* no.4150); thus appointed time, appointed place. Genesis 1:14 therefore declares that God will use the stars to communicate and signal his 'appointments' with man.

The idea of communication is repeated in Psalms: *The heavens declare the glory of God… There is no speech nor language where their voice is not heard. Their line is gone out through all the earth, and their words to the end of the world*, (Psalm 19:1-4).

Astronomy, please note. Not astrology.

We have, all of us, since childhood, heard the story of the star that led the wise men to Jesus. Rick Larson, a lawyer and amateur astronomer, has created a compelling documentary on the skyscape of 3 B.C., titled *The Star of Bethlehem*, (please google). In August 3 B.C. the two brightest planets in our solar system, Jupiter and Venus, appeared to briefly merge (as seen from earth); with Jupiter (the king planet) in Leo (the king constellation), and the sun entering Virgo, a constellation traditionally associated with the Jews. In September 3 B.C. there was a conjunction between Jupiter and Regulus (the brightest star in Leo, also called the king star). This conjunction was repeated in 2 B.C., when Jupiter in retrograde motion looped Regulus in February and again in May. On June 17, 2 B.C. Jupiter and Venus were 4 arc minutes apart, about 35° above the horizon. As the night deepened Jupiter and Venus drew closer, to within 36 arc seconds apart at an altitude of 15° above the horizon, hanging low in the sky, appearing to coalesce into a single star of immense brilliance.

Is this the star the magi saw, is this the star they followed?

The heavenly play of courtship, conception, coronation and birth described above was carried out over a ten-month period and it would make Jesus a spring baby – appropriate, too; lambs are born in the spring, (I do not think that God, so precise in all else, would have slipped up on that little detail!).

I have digressed a little from the Feasts of Our Lord to an exact year for Christ's crucifixion and birth because they are essential on the prophecy line later on. For the Feasts of Our Lord, only the religious dates are important; and, as we saw, Passover was fulfilled in precise detail. Even the selection of a lamb without blemish, four days prior to Passover, was fulfilled by Christ to the exact day when he rode into Jerusalem, hailed by the people with shouts of Alleluia and the waving of palm leaves, on Nisan 10. We now call that day Palm Sunday.

The Feast of Unleavened Bread on Nisan 15, the second feast, follows the day after Passover. Flatbread, prepared without yeast, was baked in Jewish households. This bread (matzo) was traditionally scratched over with a fork and pierced. Jewish mothers would place the flatbread in a fold of clean cloth and hide it for the children to find.

This bread, striped and pierced, is the body of our Lord Jesus Christ.

Jesus was born in Bethlehem which means, in Hebrew, 'House of Bread' (Beth Lechem). Jesus called himself *the bread of life,* (John 6:35). Bread was part of the designated sacrifice in Leviticus, the table of 'shew bread' in the tabernacle, *the bread of thy God,* (Lev.21:8).

The fork marks on the matzo are the scourge marks from the lashes that tore into our saviour's body, *with his stripes we are healed* (Isaiah 53:5); the piercings on the bread are the thorns that pierced his scalp, the sword that pierced his side, *they shall look on him whom they have pierced,* (John 19:37; Zech.12:10).

Bread baked without leaven because Jesus was without sin.

Wrapped in a cloth, the shroud.

Hidden away, in a tomb.

The second feast fulfilled, in perfect detail, to the day.

And so to the third, the Feast of First Fruits. It was to be performed *on the morrow after the Sabbath* (Lev.23:11); a sheaf of the first fruits of the harvest was to be brought to the priest to be offered to the Lord. Since, in 33 A.D., Passover was on a Friday, followed by the Saturday Sabbath, the day after would be Sunday.

[N.B. This set of three running dates would not necessarily hold good for every year, therefore a group of days for possible occurrence of this feast are provided on the Jewish calendar; this is also why 33 A.D. is the only clear date for the crucifixion of Jesus Christ, an internal validation.]

And when the Sabbath was past, Mary Magdalene, and Mary the mother of James, and Salome had brought sweet spices [to] anoint him. And very early in the morning the first day of the week, they came unto the sepulchre at the rising of the sun… they saw that the stone was rolled away…[and] a young man sitting on the right side, clothed in a long white garment; and they were affrighted. And he saith unto them, Be not affrighted: Ye seek Jesus of Nazareth which was crucified; he is risen, (Mark 16:1-6).

The resurrection.

It is on this awesome event that our faith revolves.

This is what Christ meant when he said, *Destroy this temple, and in three days I will raise it up,* (John 2:19).

Let us briefly look at the Shroud of Turin, a faith sustaining miracle reserved for our time. The shroud, a 14ft by 4ft piece of linen cloth, holds the negative image of a man who suffered the same horrendous torture inflicted on Jesus Christ as related in the gospels – the scourging, the crown of thorns, the nails of crucifixion, the spear in his side. Carbon dating tests done in 1988 gave mixed results pointing to the mid-thirteenth century; but those results, once presented as definitive, are now proven false. The sample was drawn from a repaired edge of cloth with older and newer threads in a mixed weave, typical of skilled tapestry salvage in the middle ages. Sceptics who still try to dismiss the shroud as a forgery are unable to explain the inability of twenty-first century science (or art) to replicate what was done with supposed ease in medieval times – and then hidden away, awaiting the marvel of photography to finally reveal it hundreds of years later, in 1898.

Scientists confirm that the cloth bears no pigment of any kind; but, till today, with every technological advancement at their disposal, they are unable to recreate the image-transfer mechanism of the shroud; till today, they cannot explain the 3D information delivered by this seemingly flat image, now recognised as a quantum hologram.

Dame Isabel Piczek, (1941-2016), a Hungarian particle physicist, artist and researcher, believes the Shroud of Turin has brought science to a new level of understanding in physics and quantum theory. The undistorted image on the shroud is the result of an interface that divides the image transport into two hermetically sealed areas, separate yet simultaneous, with the shroud taut and parallel on both sides and the body levitating between, creating a true event horizon. Piczek declares, 'Some believe that the tomb and shroud signify death but the exact opposite is true… the tomb signifies an unbelievable beginning because in the depth of the collapsed event horizon there is something which science knows as singularity. This is exactly what started the universe in the Big Bang. We have nothing less in the tomb of Christ than the beginning of a new universe.' [Piczek, lecture, Rome International Symposium, 1993].

Jesus is the first fruit of the resurrected dead, first among all who hope for eternal life.

In his letter to the Corinthians, Paul writes, *Now is Christ risen from the dead and become the first fruits of them that slept… Christ the first fruits; afterwards they that are Christ's at his coming,* (1Cor.15:20-23).

The Feast of First Fruits was fulfilled on the exact day assigned to it.

The fourth feast of YHWH is the Feast of Weeks. It is celebrated on Sivan 6, fifty days after the feast of First Fruits. We are provided two descriptions, *the morrow after the seventh Sabbath shall ye number fifty days,* (Lev.23:16); and later, *Seven weeks shalt thou number unto thee…And thou shall keep the feast of weeks unto the LORD thy God with the tribute of a freewill offering of thine hand,* (Deut.16:9-10).

How was this feast fulfilled by Christ?

Pentecost is celebrated exactly fifty days after Easter. It marks the descent of the Holy Spirit on the apostles (Acts 2:1-31). It is a free offering of the gifts of the spirit: wisdom and faith, fortitude and counsel, healing, prophecy and the gift of tongues. The Holy Spirit gave the apostles an unshakeable belief in their crucified leader which would transform these fishermen into fishers of men. Against all odds, this small group of disciples built the early church and transformed the world. These gifts of the Holy Spirit continue to be on offer to all God's people.

Pentecost powered forward the creation of a new religion, Christianity.

Pentecost kept alive in Christianity (especially later, when Christianity broke from its Jewish roots) the notion of jubilee, or fifty, a timespan that is important on the prophetic calendar.

Pentecost, the middle feast of seven, introduces the concept of balance and choice. The first three feasts were executed by God without man's help (or only his negative help). Pentecost works both ways: God with man, man with God; together. The notion of choice is embodied in the tribute assigned to God by this feast, *a freewill offering of thine hand.*

Choice and freewill are balancing concepts in man's destiny.

We will look at these concepts later on.

The four spring feasts are followed by three fall feasts, starting with the Feast of Trumpets, Tishri 1-2, *In the seventh month, in the first day of the month, shall ye have a Sabbath, a memorial blowing of trumpets, a holy convocation,* (Lev.23:24).

Tishri, in September-October, is the seventh month in the religious calendar but also the start of the Jewish civil year. The feast commenced at the first sighting of the new moon, even the tiniest sliver of moon; because of the difficulty (in the historic past) of quickly communicating this sighting to the full nation, informing them that the feast had begun, it became a two-day feast; because of the difficulty in knowing exactly when it would begin, an old Hebrew colloquialism associated with this feast were the words, *of that day and hour knoweth no man –*

This colloquialism appears in Christ's Olivet discourse, (Matt.24:36; Mark 13:32).

The requirement of the feast was simple: the blowing of trumpets, at intervals, over a two-day period. On a side note, this feast took place at the grain harvest and there is an instruction in Leviticus that the corners of the field be left uncut for the poor and the alien, i.e. generosity.

In the Bible, the trumpet is used primarily to call an assembly: for announcement, for religious purposes, for war. The trumpet appears in the battle of Jericho (Joshua 6:4), in Gideon's call to the people (Judges

6:34), when Saul announces victory (1Sam.13:3), when temple sacrifice is renewed under Hezekiah (2Chr.29:26-28). God himself called his people to assembly with a trumpet, *And it came to pass on the third day in the morning, that there were thunders and lightnings, and a thick cloud upon the mount, and the voice of the trumpet exceeding loud; so that all the people [in the camp] trembled. And Moses brought forth the people out of the camp to meet with God,* (Exo.19:16-17).

Trumpets are also used in warning and judgement.

The prophet is pictured as a watchman with a trumpet of warning (Jer.6:17; Eze.33:3-6).

Trumpets fill the Book of Revelation. The Elect are caught up to God with the breaking of the seventh seal and a trumpet blast; each subsequent blast announces judgement. Noteworthy, in this context, are the words of the Apostle Paul, *Behold, I shew you a mystery; We shall not all sleep, but we shall all be changed, In a moment, in the twinkling of an eye, at the last trump: for the trumpet shall sound, and the dead shall be raised incorruptible, and we shall be changed,* (1Cor.15:51-52).

Does this feast herald the Gathering of the Elect, commonly called the Rapture?

Atonement, Tishri 10, is the sixth feast. It is the highest of holy days: *Also on the tenth day of this seventh month, there shall be a day of atonement: it shall be an holy convocation unto you; and ye shall afflict your souls, and offer an offering made by fire unto the LORD,* (Lev.23:27).

Work is forbidden on this day, it is solely for the contemplation of sins committed.

As the awesome Feast of Atonement ends, the Jews conduct a ceremony called Neilah, which means 'closing the gate'; the slowly closing door symbolises that the future is sealed. The metaphor of a door is one associated with Jesus who called himself the door for the sheep, the door of life, *I am the door: by me if any man enter in, he shall be saved, and shall go in and out and find pasture,* (John 10:9). And again, *Enter ye in at the strait gate…Because strait is the gate and narrow is the way which leadeth unto life, and few there be that find it,* (Matt.7:13-14).

A door, closing in one's face, is an unsettling image; even fearful.

The message is simple –

If repentance is sincere, it permits passage; if not, not.

Jesus is not only represented as the door of life but also as holding the key of David, *And the key of the house of David will I lay upon his shoulder; so he shall open, and none shall shut; and he shall shut, and none shall open. And I will fasten him as a nail in a sure place,* (Isaiah 22:22-23). This verse is echoed in Revelation, the words spoken by Jesus himself, *These things saith he that is holy, he that is true, he that hath the key of David, he that openeth and no man shutteth; and shutteth and no man openeth,* (Rev.3:7).

What key?

In Hebrew, David is written with just three letters, DVD. In the paleo-Hebraic script (which we will look at next), 'D' was written like a tipsy triangle, meaning door; 'V' was written like an inverted tent-peg (Y), meaning nail. Thus David means door-nail-door. If the two triangles 'D' that comprise David are fastened with a nail 'V', the 'nail' creates a tetrahedron, and the two locked triangles become a star (figure iv); this is the origin of the Star of David.

Jesus, the *root and offspring of David* (Rev.22:16), is both door and key, controlling passage.

If the fall feasts play out as the spring ones did, then the timespan between Trumpets and Atonement is for those who were not among the Elect, that they may yet repent and be saved. Jesus will judge passage

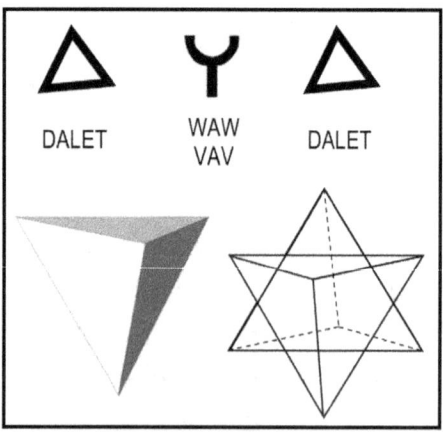

Fig. iv: Tetrahedron and the Key of David

through the closing door. He says, *I am he which searcheth the reins and hearts: and I will give unto every one of you according to your works,* (Rev.2:23). And again, *I know thy works: behold, I have set before thee an open door, and no man can shut it: for thou hast a little strength, and hast kept my word, and hast not denied my name,* (Rev.3:8).

The Feast of Tabernacles, Tishri 15-22, is the seventh and last feast: *The fifteenth day of this seventh month shall be the feast of tabernacles for seven days unto the LORD,* (Lev.23:34). During this feast the Jewish people were to gather in Jerusalem, *Men and women and children, and thy stranger that is within thy gates, that they may hear and that they may learn, and fear the LORD your God,* (Deut.31:12).

It is a solemn but joyous feast.

It is the longest feast, lasting seven days.

It is the only feast where God commanded an inclusion of the Gentiles. The promise to the Gentiles, made apparent here, is repeated in Isaiah in a messianic promise, *And he said it is a light thing that thou shouldest be my servant to raise up the tribes of Jacob, and to restore the preserved of Israel: I will also give thee for a light to the Gentiles, that thou mayest be my salvation unto the end of the earth,* (Isaiah 49:6).

This feast acknowledges the protection of God, remembering his provision in the wilderness and his sheltering arm in this world. It is celebrated by Jews today with tent-like structures set up on balconies or in backyards, in commemoration of the tents in the desert. It is a favourite time for Jewish weddings.

An event of prophetic parallelism, central to this feast, is told in that most tender of love stories, the Book of Ruth. Ruth, the Moabite, newly widowed, joins her mother-in-law, Naomi, in a journey back to Naomi's land. They arrive at harvest time, seeking sustenance, stumbling by chance upon the field of Naomi's kinsman, Boaz. Naomi makes known to Ruth the traditions by which Ruth claims Boaz and his protection; through Ruth, Naomi wins security. It is a shadow enactment: Boaz/Christ as kinsman-Redeemer; Naomi/Israel; Ruth/the Church.

Interestingly, Ruth is a gentile.

She arrives at the time of gleaning (significant to the story, associated with the Feast of Trumpets).

Boaz is a direct line ancestor of David, his great-grandfather: Boaz-Obed-Jesse-David.

Significantly, in Genesis 38:9-30, in a passage referencing the house of Judah, appear the names of Boaz-Ruth-Obed-Jesse(Yishay)-David, at a skip of 49 letters, in chronological order, (see Daniel Michelson, *Codes in the Torah*). Ruth's inclusion in a line of male 'seed' is unusual and prophetic.

Some prophecy teachers link the Feast of Tabernacles to the Wedding of the Lamb (Rev.19:7);

others equate it with the start of God's millennial kingdom on earth (Rev.21:2), when God will tabernacle with man in a New Jerusalem.

The fall feasts have yet to happen, we can only guess at their fulfilment; but they will be fulfilled on their due dates, at a time of God's choosing.

Probably during the last days, that zone best fits Trumpets and Atonement.

What is clear from the order of the feasts is that God has done his bit during the spring feasts; Pentecost has swung the pendulum towards us. We must repent where required, correct as necessary, endure if we are on the right path. What happens during the fall feasts will be based on our commitment and the choices we make NOW.

Faith and action are both required.

Not every one that saith unto me, Lord, Lord, shall enter into the kingdom of heaven, but he that doeth the will of my Father which is in heaven, (Matt.7:21)

But be ye doers of the Word, and not hearers only, (James 1:22).

Wherefore by their fruits ye shall know them, (Matt.7:20).

We are saved by grace and only by grace.

But, once saved, we will be judged according to our works.

3 – Names

The timeline of the Genesis Patriarchs is used by Bible scholars to draw an exact measurement of years from Adam to Jacob, 2255 years later. After that the line squiggles a bit till Exodus and the firmer (biblical) ground of the entry into Canaan.

You have probably read and dismissed those numbers as fiction.

Maybe you have not read them at all.

No matter, this chapter does not deal with Genesis timelines but with names and the meaning of those names. Did you know that the pre-Flood patriarchs have a story to tell?

This one:

Adam	…	man
Seth	…	appointed (to)
Enosh	…	mortal
Kenan	…	sorrow
Mahalalel	…	the Blessed God

Jared	...	shall come down
Enoch	...	teaching/dedicated
Methuselah	...	his death shall bring
Lamech	...	the despairing
Noah	...	rest/comfort

It is a prophecy on man and his salvation, a redemptive plan revealed through the direct descent line of the Genesis patriarchs, a fascinating gem uncovered by Dr. Charles Missler in his essay, *A Hidden Message: The Gospel in Genesis*, February 1996. Beyond the prophecy laid out in the names of these men is a deeper truth: the Bible proclaims itself as a cohesive, multilayered body of work, conceived in precise detail, waiting to yield its treasure to the one who seeks.

Names are intrinsic to communication and in all languages names have meaning.

But Hebrew goes a step further.

Each letter of the Hebrew alphabet steps beyond its alphanumeric qualities to function as a pictogram. We had a sneak preview of this aspect when we touched on the name David.

The ancient paleo-Hebraic script offers a language of pictures with associated meanings – for example, the letter A/aleph appears in paleo-Hebrew as an ox head, meaning chief or leader, also strength and pre-eminence; B/beit is pictured as a tent, meaning house, also household and family (figure v). Pictures can

Fig. v: Paleo-Hebrew script with equivalent letters, values and meanings

thus be formed within a name from the letters which comprise that name, disclosing additional aspects to that name, enhancing understanding.

Let us look at a few names –

Starting with His Most Holy Name, YHWH.

This is the name that God delivered to Moses in Exodus, when Moses asked, *who shall I say sent me? And God said unto Moses, I AM THAT I AM: and he said, Thus shalt thou say unto the children of Israel, I AM hath sent me unto you,* (Exo.3:14).

In the Hebrew text, the words I AM THAT I AM appear as the word YHWH, a name so holy that it is never spoken aloud by the Jewish people but is replaced by the word Adonai; English translations carry the word LORD, in capitals. The holy tetragrammaton YHWH is drawn from the verb Hayâh, to be, (*Strong's Concordance* no.1961), and contains in its Hebraic script every tense of the verb 'to be': past, present and future – was, is, will be.

It is a statement of eternal existence.

This statement of eternal existence appears in the simple prayer, As it was in the beginning is now and ever shall be, world without end, Amen.

This statement of eternal existence appears throughout the Bible; in the books of praise and in the prophets; in Job and in Ecclesiastes; in Isaiah, *Remember the former things of old: for I am God, and there is none else; I am God and there is none like me, Declaring the end from the beginning and from ancient times the things which are not yet done,* (Isaiah 46:9-10); and in Colossians, *All things were created by him and for him: And he is before all things, and by him all things consist,* (Col.1:16-17).

The I AM declaration of Exodus recalls the seven great I AMs of John's gospel, paralleled by the seven great I AMs of Revelation, used by Jesus to identify aspects of himself.

Once again, the number seven.

In the gospel of John: *I am the bread of life (6:35), I am the light of the world (8:12), I am the door of the sheep (10:7), I am the good shepherd (10:11), I am the resurrection and the life (11:25), I am the way, the truth and the life (14:6), I am the true vine (15:1).*

And in the Book of Revelation: *I am Alpha and Omega (thrice, 1:8, 1:11, 22:13), I am the first and the last (1:17), I am alive forevermore (1:18), I am he which searcheth the reins and hearts (2:23), I am the root and the offspring of David (22:16).*

[N.B. The other I AMs of John, not listed above, do not appear in the original Greek text but are added in translations.]

How must this Holy Name be pronounced?

Since the Hebrew alphabet is comprised almost exclusively of consonants with the vowel component (necessary for pronunciation) a remembered sound relayed by common usage, and since the word YHWH was too holy to speak aloud, (uttered only once a year by the high priest on the Day of Atonement), the exact pronunciation of this word as given to Moses has passed from exact memory. It is now variously represented by rabbinical scholars as Ya-ho-wah, Ya-hu-wah, Yah-weh.

Given the fact that the Old and New Testament are locked together, should this lack of a definitive pronunciation for so vastly important a name trouble us? The surprising answer is no, and the reason lies in the pictograms which exemplify this Holy Name.

They are:

Y (yud), hand or arm, meaning control/power, responsibility

H (heh), man with arms raised, meaning revelation, behold/see

W (w/vav), nail/tent peg, meaning fasten/connect

H (heh) as above, behold/see

And now, with these four pictograms, a huge and incredible truth becomes apparent, (figure vi):

YHWH means, Hand-Behold-Nail-Behold

It is the story of Christ nailed to the cross.

It is the story of salvation.

A poignant passage in the New Testament paints an exact picture of this name. It is after the resurrection; Jesus appears to his disciples in a locked room – but one disciple, Thomas, is not present; when the other disciples tell Thomas the wondrous news he will not

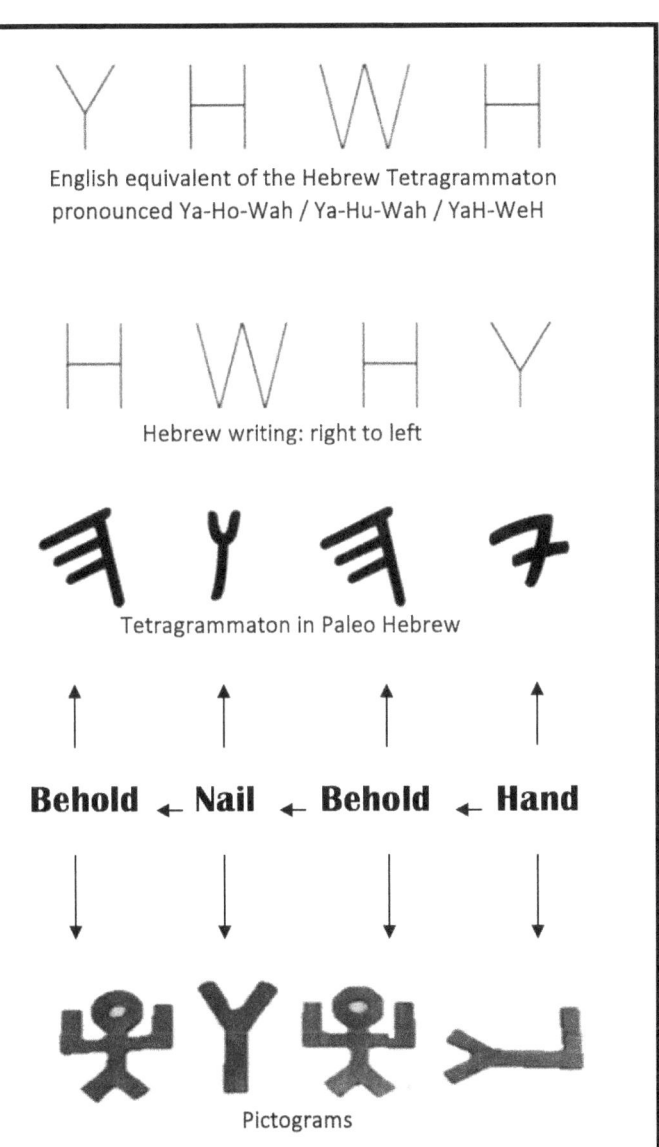

Fig. vi: The Holy Tetragrammaton, YHWH

believe; Thomas declares, *Except I shall see in his hands the print of the nails, and put my finger into the print of the nails, and thrust my hand into his side, I will not believe,* (John 20:25). Eight days later the disciples are again together and Thomas is with them. Jesus appears once again. He says to his doubting disciple, *Thomas, Reach hither thy finger, and behold my hands; and reach hither thy hand, and thrust it into my side: and be not faithless but believing. And Thomas answered and said unto him, My Lord and my God. Jesus saith unto him, Thomas, because thou hast seen me thou hast believed: blessed are they that have not seen and yet have believed,* (John 20:27-29).

YHWH and Jesus, are they the same?

Let us return to Genesis 1:1, but this time I will group the Bible's opening verse into seven words as they appear in the original Hebrew (figure vii):

<u>In the beginning</u>   <u>created</u>   <u>God</u>   <u>Aleph Tav</u>
<u>heavens</u>   <u>and the</u>   <u>earth</u>

Fig. vii: The seven words comprising Hebrew Genesis 1:1, Aleph Tav at center

Aleph Tav, what is that word?

Where did it come from?

The word at the center of this first sentence in the original Masoretic Text never appears in any translation. It is, in fact, untranslatable without an extended phrase; and because aleph is a silent 'A' needing consonants on either side to shape the sound, it cannot be pronounced without linkage. Due to the curious structure of Hebrew grammar, the verb 'created' precedes the subject 'God' – thus Aleph Tav, following God, appears to name God, or to name a quality of God.

What does Aleph Tav mean?

The pictorial value of Aleph has been given at the start of this chapter as pre-eminent, leader. Tav is the last letter of the Hebrew alphabet; the pictogram is of two crossed sticks, meaning mark or seal, also sign and covenant (figure viii).

Aleph Tav together thus means leader-covenant, strength-seal, pre-eminent-mark, chief-cross. The letters carry the first number aleph = 1, and highest value Tav = 400; positioned at the start and at the end of the Hebrew alphabet, they are the equivalent of saying A to Z.

The pictograms deliver a powerful message.

Aleph Tav exactly matches the description Jesus gives of himself in Revelation, *I am Alpha and Omega, the beginning and the end, the first and the last,*

Fig. viii: Aleph Tav, revealed through pictogram

(Rev.22:13). He is on the last page of the Bible what he declared himself on the first, Creator and Redeemer. He made a covenant with his people and sealed it. The crossed sticks of Tav represent the cross of Christ; the crossed sticks of Tav also signify the covenant. The covenant promised salvation; 'salvation' in Hebrew is spelled Yeshua/Jesus.

The covenant and cross, the saviour and salvation.

Aleph Tav and Jesus, are they the same?

By extension, are Aleph Tav and YHWH the same?

Aleph Tav and YHWH have no apparent link in the Old Testament (or if linked, the link is not clear), but they are directly linked in pictorial representation to Jesus Christ, the promised Messiah of the Old Testament, fulfilled in the New. Salvation, the promise of the covenant, was made possible by Jesus nailed to the cross. Refused, rejected – but still on offer; a promise of salvation which will be delivered in full to all who believe in Jesus on the last day.

The image of a cross dominates the New Testament. But it also appears in the Old: hidden in Exodus, elucidated in Numbers.

The Israelites, as they wandered through the wilderness, were carefully instructed as to the layout of the camp around the tabernacle of God which housed the Ark of the Covenant. Each tribe with their princely leader had precise positions (Num.2:2-34). At night, seen from above, the tents with their campfires would have looked like a huge lighted cross moving slowly towards the Promised Land (figure ix).

Curiously enough, the banners of the four lead tribes for each section were: (i) east, Judah, lion; (ii) south, Reuben, man; (iii) west, Ephraim, ox; (iv) north, Dan, eagle. These are the faces of the four living creatures about the throne of God, as described by John in Revelation (Rev.4:7).

At the heart of this cross lies the tabernacle with the Ark of the Covenant. The Ark was built to hold the Ten Commandments, the law written on stone and given to Moses. The Tablets of Testimony were broken by Moses when he saw the Israelites dancing around the golden calf; but they were fashioned anew (Exo.34:4) symbolising a second chance.

Some dismiss the Ten Commandments as Old Testament.

Jesus is love, they declare.

And this is indisputably true.

But Jesus also said, *Think not that I am come to destroy the law, or the prophets: I am come not to destroy but to fulfil. For verily I say unto you, Till heaven and earth pass, one jot or one tittle shall in no wise pass from the law till all be fulfilled,* (Matt.5:17-18). In fact each of the ten commandments is validated in the New

NAMES | **63**

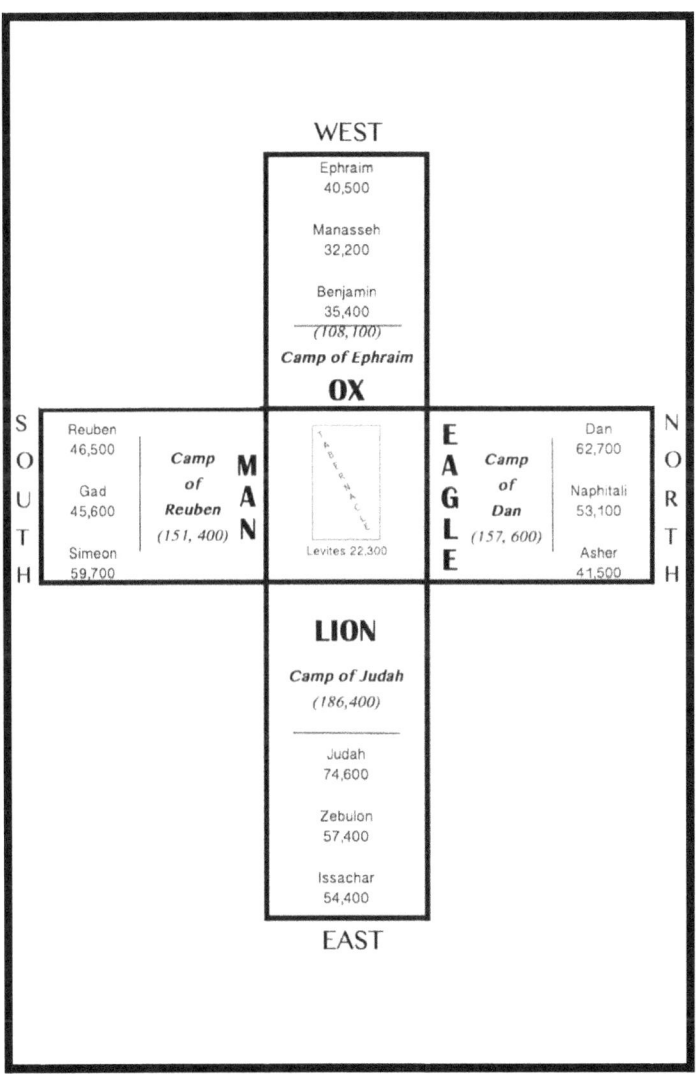

Fig. ix: Cross in the Desert; the Living Creatures about the Throne of God

Testament: Matt.4:10; 1John 5:21; 1Tim.6:1; Mark 2:27; Matt.19:19; Rom.13:9; Matt.19:8; Eph.4:20; Rom.13:9; Rom.7:7 (only single instances provided here).

The Old and New Testaments are truly locked together.

Let us delve into the name 'Jesus' a little more, touching upon his multiple attributes and the names he assigns himself. Because at one level the Bible is math, we will return briefly to numerics:

Two numbers repeatedly appear with the names of Jesus Christ, 8 and 37.

8 is the number of resurrection or new life.

37 is the numeric value for *life*.

Jesus started his ministry at the age of thirty and his ministry lasted three and a half years. He completed a mortal lifespan of thirty-three and a half years. Does '37' suggest that three and a half years will yet be completed by Jesus in some form? Does the number three and a half appear anywhere in the Bible?

It does, in Daniel and in the Book of Revelation.

In both books, it refers to a period of great tribulation, before the Second Coming of Christ.

Stellarium is planetarium software which may be downloaded off the internet; it allows the user to create a skyscape on a computer screen with realistic

Jesus	...	888 = 8x111
Christ	...	1480 = 8x185
Jesus Christ	...	2368 = 8x296
Son of Man	...	2960 = 8x370
Lord	...	800 = 8x100
Godhead	...	592 = 8x74
Messiah	...	656 = 8x82
Saviour	...	1408 = 8x176

Jesus	...	888 = 37x8x3
Christ	...	1480 = 37x8x5
Jesus Christ	...	2368 = 37x8x8
Son of Man	...	2960 = 37x8x10
Lord of Hosts	...	1813 = 37x7x7
Godhead	...	592 = 37x8x2
Christ our Passover	...	3700 = 37x10x10
Life	...	37 = 37

3D imaging. The app uses the precise math of Kepler's laws and permits travel forwards and backwards in time, tracking the movement of the heavenly bodies during any year for any given day. Using this app, Bible scholar Scott Clarke detected a rare planetary configuration exactly representing the heavenly wonder of Rev. 12:1-2; his stunning discovery has since been analysed by prophecy watchers in minute detail. The star map will come into precise alignment on September 23, 2017.

How rare is rare?

Rare as in never before or again, once only.

On December 23, 2016, Jupiter entered the constellation Virgo, lodging in the belly of the constellation and remaining there for 38 weeks (moving in retrograde motion, as seen from earth). Thirty-eight weeks is the gestational period of a human baby.

[N.B. Common representation of Virgo shows the torso as a four-sided quadrangle; but finer depictions of the torso indicate a small indentation on the image's left side, making the torso a five-sided polygon. Jupiter enters through this indented area on December 23, 2016.]

On September 9, 2017 Jupiter slowly exits the belly of the constellation. On September 23, 2017 as Jupiter passes between the legs of the constellation towards full exit, the other parts of Revelation 12 come into play: the planets (also known as wandering stars) Mercury, Mars and Venus join the nine main stars of the constellation Leo, above the head of Virgo, to form a crown of twelve stars; at the same time the sun is at the shoulder of Virgo, 'clothing' her; and the moon is by her feet –

And there appeared a great wonder in heaven, a

woman clothed with the sun, and the moon under her feet, and upon her head a crown of twelve stars: And she being with child cried, travailing in birth, (Rev.12:1-2; figure x).

This 'wonder' opens John's vision of the tribulation as seen from earth.

Let us consider this star map with critical doubt.

Is it truly rare? Is it a sign?

To put matters in perspective, let us examine the routine:

(i) the sun passes through Virgo once every year, between August and October, 'clothing' her;

(ii) Virgo carries Messier 87 in the head region of the constellation; it is a supergiant elliptical galaxy

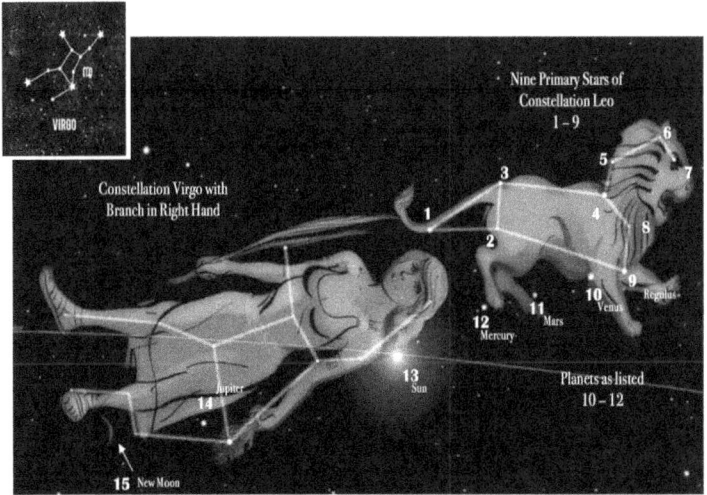

Fig. x: Star map, Book of Revelation 12:1

with twelve thousand globular clusters of stars circling a black hole, giving the appearance of a crown or halo; this crown is there every day, always; however if we seek a crown beyond this continuous event (as suggested by the word 'sign'), then the planets Venus, Mars and Mercury align with the stars of Leo once every eight/nine years; this view draws Leo (the king constellation), Regulus (the king star) and Jupiter (the king planet) into a triple confirmation of 'royalty'; Leo also links symbolically to the lion of Judah;

(iii) every nineteenth year the moon will be in the region of the constellation's 'feet' while the sun is 'clothing' her;

(iv) Jupiter passes every twelfth year through Virgo but only once every eighty-three years does it move in retrograde motion for 37-42 weeks within (or approximately within) the torso.

The movements of these heavenly bodies are thus not exceptional in themselves – yet if we track backwards through time this astronomical convergence has never happened before.

Travelling forward, it does not happen either.

What is exceptional is the alignment of these individual events, converging together to create the star map of September 23, 2017.

And there appeared a great wonder –

[N.B. The KJV translates the word as 'wonder'; most editions render the easier word, 'sign'; the same

Greek word appears in Revelation 15:1 as 'sign'; it should be noted that this is the only time the Bible identifies a sign as 'great.']

Until the recent past, this passage in Revelation was taken to reference the birth of our saviour, two thousand years ago, with Herod and his slaughter of the Innocents in the role of *great red dragon*, (Rev.12:3) – and in a broad sense, this interpretation is also true, major prophecies often hold a dual fulfilment. But, while recalling the birth of Jesus, this is not the meaning of this prophetic text: Christ's birth is in the past, behind John; Revelation, by its very nature, looks ahead to something unknown, revealing it. The Book of Revelation explicitly states itself as a revelation of the last days.

The sign, then, is tied to the last days.

It may be noted here that the September convergence is preceded by a total solar eclipse. On August 21, 2017 the sun, moon and earth will be in perfect syzygy; the path of totality will cross the United States from Oregon to South Carolina with a maximum duration of 2 minutes, 41 seconds.

An important insight on Revelation 12 is provided by the work of Michael Svigel, (Department Chair and Professor of Theological Studies, Dallas Theological Seminary) in his study of the Greek word for 'child'. The child of Revelation 12 appears under different nomenclature in the original Greek text, *And the dragon stood before the woman... for to devour her child[1] before it was born. And she brought forth a man child[2] who was to rule all nations with a rod of iron: and her child[3] was caught up to God and to his throne,* (Rev.12:4-5).

The Greek word 'teknon' (*Strong's Concordance* no.G5043), is used for child[1] and child[3]; it is a figurative use of child (either sex), meaning descendant, inhabitant (as in John 1:12, children of God; Ephesians 5:8, children of light; 1 Peter 1:14, children of flesh; Galatians 4:28, children of promise). The Greek word 'huios' (*Strong's Concordance* no.G5207), is used for child[2]; it carries the meaning of son, descendant, stressing resemblance and inheritance; 'huios' appears in every New Testament reference to Jesus (as in Son of Man, Son of God, Son of David; as in Hebrews 1:2, *Hath in these last days spoken unto us by his Son, whom he hath appointed heir of all things*).

The duality of 'child', exposed through the original Greek text, heightens the portent of this sign.

The three 'wandering star' planets add to the star map: Venus, linked to the Jewish people; Mars signifying violence/war linked to the antichrist; Mercury, the messenger.

Does the messenger bring a message?

As the Star of Bethlehem announced Christ's birth, does this star pattern speak, too?

But first, a STRONG CAUTION: Jesus does NOT appear on earth (not in person, not by hologram, not by astral projection) during this time. It is a representation, through the heavenly bodies which are ordered by God, telling those who wait for him that his coming is near, that he is with us, hovering above. Jesus warned his disciples two thousand years ago against false christs who would appear during the period of tribulation, using deception to advance their claims. Please know that Jesus will only return in earth shattering splendour on the last day, riding on clouds of glory (Matt.24:30), stepping onto the Mount of Olives (Zech.14:4), and, with the breath of his mouth, destroying the armies of evil gathered at Armageddon (Rev.16:16).

To return to the star map of Revelation –

There are three possibilities, all valid.

First, the configuration marks the midpoint of tribulation. This analysis offers the shortest timeline (three and a half years) and presupposes that we are already in tribulation (as some would agree). September 2017, as midpoint, necessitates a start date of April 2014. This is the month in which the first blood moon of the blood moon tetrad of 2014-2015 appeared; the blood moons falling precisely on the Feasts of Passover and Tabernacles, the series punctuated by four solar eclipses. The 2014-2015 tetrad was the ninth tetrad from and including the crucifixion year 32-33 A.D. (9, the number of finality and judgement). Following the 'wonder,' the woman flees *to a place prepared of God, that they should feed her there a thousand two hundred and threescore days,* (Rev.12:6); lending credence to the midpoint theory, the period from the first blood moon (April 15, 2014) to the heavenly sign (Sept 23, 2017) is 1,258 days.

Second, the configuration marks the start of a seven-year period of tribulation. This supposition is an equally strong contender and favoured by many scholars who see the prophecy pieces falling into place but not yet fully aligned. In this timeline, Christ – to complete the balance three and a half years suggested by the 'life' numeric – would appear midway during tribulation. This could tie in with John's vision of the Lamb on Mount Sion (Rev.14:1), which precedes the trumpet plagues.

Third, the configuration marks the start of an extended ten-year period of 'generation' (Matt.24:34, more on this later); this is a weaker contender, but also valid when we use the stopwatch principle of prophecy. This principle is established by the still unfinished Seventy Weeks of Daniel; it is also validated by Jesus Christ when he reads from the scroll of Isaiah, in Nazareth, *The Spirit of the Lord God is upon me; because the LORD hath appointed me to preach the gospel to the poor; he hath sent me to heal the broken hearted, to preach deliverance to the captives, and recovering of sight to the blind, to set at liberty them that are bruised, To preach the acceptable year of the LORD,* (Luke 4:18-19). Jesus halts at this point. He halts in the middle of a sentence. The second half of that same sentence in Isaiah is, *and the day of vengeance of our God*, (Isaiah 61:2). Jesus presses the stopwatch because he came in mercy; the day of vengeance is reserved for end times.

This book does not set dates.

But it confirms a zone.

The precise convergence of select heavenly bodies on September 23, 2017 into the star map 'birth' sign heralds a period prophesized about through the ages, *And I will shew wonders in the heavens… the sun shall be turned into darkness, and the moon into blood, before the great and the terrible day of the LORD come,* (Joel 2:30-31).

Coincidently, this day appears on the Hebrew calendar as 'Shabbat Shuva' or the Sabbath of Return.

4 – Daniel, the visions

Daniel is not included among the major or even minor prophets of the Jewish Tanakh, his work is relegated to the last division of Hebrew Canon, called 'the writings'; but the Church esteems Daniel as a pre-eminent prophet of the Old Testament, one of the greatest, whose visions provide the most comprehensive statement of future events found anywhere in the Bible. It is in Daniel that the rise and fall of kingdoms is foretold and the play of end times is laid out. It is Christ himself who directs our attention to Daniel (Matt.24:15) when he discusses the period of tribulation which will precede his Second Coming.

We will start, as always, at the beginning.

The beginning, for Daniel, is around 605 B.C.; it is the third year of Jehoiakim, king of Judah (609/8-598 B.C) and the first year of Nebuchadnezzar, king of Babylon (605-562 B.C.).

Nebuchadnezzar is continuing the battles of his father Nabopolassar against the smaller, neighbouring kingdoms and Judah is under attack (there will be three sieges; Jerusalem and the First Temple will be destroyed over the next several years, a judgement prophesized by Jeremiah). Daniel is carried off to Babylon with the first wave of captives but because of his youth and noble descent he is admitted into the king's palace for training as a 'wise man.' Despite his captive status, Daniel adheres strictly to the law of God; for this reason, he is favoured by God and showered with prophetic greatness.

The angel will later declare, *O Daniel, I am now come forth to give thee skill and understanding… for thou art greatly beloved: therefore understand the matter, and consider the vision,* (ch.9:23).

The Book of Daniel is filled with fascinating stories: Daniel in the lion's den, the king's madness, the Jewish compatriots in the burning furnace, Belshazzar's feast and the writing on the wall, the lustful elders and Daniel's defence of innocence (the story likened to the wisdom of Solomon).

This chapter will only look at the visions.

Daniel's rise to greatness in the kingdom of Nebuchadnezzar begins with the king's dream.

Nebuchadnezzar, king of Babylon, dreams a dream which troubles him. He summons his wise men and asks that they reveal both his dream and its meaning. Quite naturally they demur – Tell us your dream, O king, and we will explain it. But Nebuchadnezzar is a wily man. *The thing is gone from me,* (ch.2:5), he declares and he renews his demand with a warning, *if ye make not known unto me the dream, with the interpretation thereof, ye shall be cut in pieces,* (ch.2:5).

It is a dire threat.

And, in those days, a very real one.

The wise men attempt to reason with the king: no man can know another's dream, they declare, no one but God. But their reasoning does not appeal to Nebuchadnezzar. He is furious and orders the death of all the wise men in his kingdom.

Daniel, as a wise man in training, is also subject to this order. He prays to God for enlightenment and in a vision is shown both the king's dream and its meaning (figure xi). Daniel asks to be taken to the king. Before a hushed court he tells Nebuchadnezzar that the king had dreamed of a mighty statue: the head of gold, chest of silver, belly and thighs of bronze, the legs of iron ending in feet of iron and clay which 'do not mix.' A stone is flung upon the statue's feet and the entire statue shatters, turning to chaff in the wind; but the stone grows into a mighty mountain which fills the whole earth.

Daniel proceeds to explain the dream. The head of gold is the current empire of Babylon. It will be followed by one of lesser splendour represented by silver, then lesser still represented by bronze, and finally a kingdom represented by iron, a kingdom which will

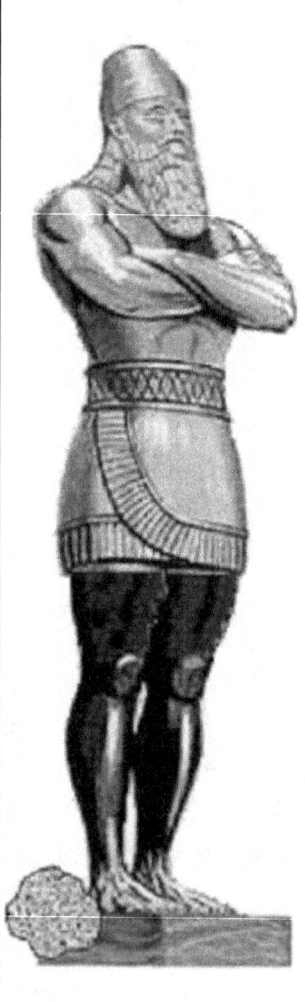

1. **Head of Gold**
   - Babylon (606 – 538 B.C.)
   - Winged Lion

2. **Breast and Arms of Silver**
   - Medo-Persia (538 – 330 B.C.)
   - Hunchbacked Bear
   - Ram with Uneven Horns

3. **Belly and Thighs of Bronze**
   - Greece (330 – 160 B.C.)
   - Four-Headed Leopard
   - Goat with Four Horns

4. **Legs of Iron**
   - Rome (160 B.C. – 476 A.D.)
   - Dreadful Beast with Ten Horns
   - Subsequent Division
     - West: Roman Empire
     - East: Byzantine Empire (Later: Ottoman Empire)

5. **Feet of Iron and Clay Mixed**
   - Morphed Roman Empire
   - End Time Empire of Anti-Christ

6. **Stone Cut Without Hands**
   - Jesus Christ
   - Millennial Reign

Fig. xi: The statue of king Nebuchadnezzar's dream

divide and change, but not die. In the last days, the morphed kingdom of iron and clay is destroyed by a supernatural force, *a stone cut without hands,* (ch.2:34). This stone will usher in the everlasting kingdom of God.

Then Nebuchadnezzar bows low before Daniel, saying, *Of a truth it is that your God is a God of gods, and a Lord of kings, and a revealer of secrets, seeing thou couldst reveal this secret,* (ch.2:47).

Daniel is raised to high position and great honour.

This first vision of Daniel is more often called the king's dream.

Daniel's second vision occurs many years after the first, in the first year of Belshazzar (556-539 B.C.; Belshazzar was co-regent with his father king Nabodinus, in complete control for the final three years 541-539 B.C.), king of Babylon, a descendant of Nebuchadnezzar.

Daniel is woken from his sleep by a vision. He sees a sea blown upon by angry winds and four animals rise out of the sea: the first is a lion with eagle's wings, but its wings are plucked, it is raised on its hind legs and the heart of a man is given to it; the second animal is a bear, the back hunched on one side and three ribs in its mouth, it is told to devour much flesh; the third is a winged leopard with four heads and dominion is given to it; the fourth is not likened to any animal but is described as a 'dreadful beast' (ch.7:7), with iron teeth and ten horns, and as Daniel watched a little horn appeared amid the others, uprooting three of them. The little horn had eyes and a mouth which uttered blasphemy. Daniel then sees the 'Ancient of Days' (ch.7:13), seated on a throne of judgement. The dreadful beast is destroyed by fire in His presence, and honour is given to the Son of Man who appears before the throne of judgement; honour, glory and an everlasting kingdom.

An angel, standing by the throne of God, tells Daniel, *These great beasts which are four, are four kings which shall arise out of the earth,* (ch.7:17).

This vision, in the seventh chapter of the Book of Daniel, occupies a unique place in biblical prophecy. It lays bare the future, drawing the outline of kingdoms yet to come, tracing a course through four great world empires (Babylon, Medo-Persia, Greece and Rome), concluding in judgement and the eternal kingdom of God.

The vision builds on the king's dream.

The animals link to the metal of the statue and its body parts. The empires are not yet mentioned by name (this will only happen in the third vision); but with our knowledge of history we will list them here for greater clarity –

Thus, the lion is Babylon, the head of gold: as the

lion is first among animals, so is Babylon first in this end-time chain of kingdoms. The winged lion was a prominent feature of the Ishtar Gate, main entranceway to the capital city Babylon; the winged lion was a companion figure and symbol of Ishtar, goddess of war and sex, including man-animal copulation, daughter of Sin, the moon god, and forerunner of Astarte. Gold was the common currency of the Babylonian empire.

The bear is the Medo-Persian kingdom which followed: the hunched back, like the statue's arms folded one over the other, suggest an unequal alliance. This is historically true: the Medes were initially more powerful than the Persians, the Persians surpassed the Medes later on. The three ribs in the bear's mouth represent the three military campaigns fought by this empire in its expansion: Lidia (Turkey), Babylon (Iraq-Iran) and Egypt. Trade was conducted chiefly in silver.

The leopard represents the Greek empire. This swiftest of all land animals epitomises the speed of Alexander the Great's conquests. The bronze of the statue matches the bronze armour favoured by the Greeks. Bronze coinage, first started in 407 B.C. by Athens, now passes into commercial use; the grain barter system is transformed into a fully integrated giro system and a central bank (the first of its kind) is established in Alexandria.

The dreadful beast is Rome: the iron teeth equate the iron breastplates and shields of the Roman soldiers, the trampling feet speak of crushing power. The divided legs of the statue foretell the division of this empire into west and east, Rome and Constantinople; one transforming into the power of the Church; the Byzantine half eventually falling to the Ottoman empire, becoming an Islamic stronghold; both finally mingling with 'common clay,' ordinary man.

The vision expands beyond a simple timeline to reveal layers of prophecy.

As the empires come and go, the metal representing each period in time decreases in value but increases in 'brutish' strength, as iron is harder than bronze, bronze harder than silver, gold the most precious and malleable of all; the devolution represents a coarsening of the human psyche.

Also important: the animal-empires link to their representative body parts, rounding out a thematic message – thus the trampling feet signify 'world' control through violence; the bronze belly is fed and controlled through 'world' commerce (the first central bank at Alexandria); the arms control through 'world' administration (Medo-Persia, the first ancient empire of extensive landmass); the head is filled with prideful hubris and the urge to self-deify, the serpent's subtle lure *ye shall be as gods* (Gen.3:5; the image of pure gold which Nebuchadnezzar builds of himself in the plain of Dura, sixty cubits in height, before which all his subjects, 'the world', must worship on pain of death, Dan.3:1-6).

The vision is a preview of the Book of Revelation, condensed and cryptic.

Daniel hears the angel speak but he does not fully understand; and he is amazed by the fourth beast and the little horn, what do they mean?

The angel explains the strangeness of the fourth beast as a kingdom *diverse from all the others [which] shall devour the whole earth,* (ch.7:23); i.e. it will not look like the kingdoms of old but it will exercise the despotic authority of those ancient kingdoms and it will encompass all humanity. 'Diverse' and 'devour' are dual elements of the final beast kingdom; they indicate a single world power with a network of complicit institutions, represented by the ten horns, which will command and control all aspects of life in the last days.

The little horn, of course, is the antichrist.

It is the first appearance of the antichrist and some qualities are assigned to this man:

- he shall speak great words against the most High
- he shall wear out the saints of the most High
- he shall seek to change times and laws
- he shall have power for a time and times and the dividing of time

A period of power is laid out for the rule of the antichrist, *time, times and the dividing of time,* (ch.7:25) which is subsequently shown as three and a half years.

During this time he will harass and persecute the followers of Jesus Christ. The angel consoles Daniel by telling him that the power of the antichrist will be totally destroyed and the greatness of the kingdom will pass to the people of God who will *possess the kingdom for ever, even for ever and ever,* (ch.7:18).

Daniel understands; but, understanding, he grieves. He writes, *My countenance changed in me: but I kept the matter in my heart.*

Daniel's third vision contains the first prophecy with a direct timeline. We will therefore take a brief timeout from the visions to discuss values assigned to certain prophetic utterances in the Bible.

Some prophecies are a straight count of days or years, as the first two examples below; other prophecies are cloaked, yielding their meaning only after labour, examples three and four. As always, in our search for prophetic meaning, we require the validation of at least two witnesses.

(i) the day as a day: as in Revelation, *And the woman fled into the wilderness, where she hath a place prepared of God, that they should feed her there a thousand two hundred and three score days,* (Rev.12:6). The validity of the straight count is borne out by this same number of three and a half years being presented in different ways, as *forty and two months* (Rev.13:5), *time, times and the dividing of time* (Dan.7:25), *a time, times and half a time* (Rev.12:14).

(ii) the year as a year: as in Jeremiah, *And this whole land shall be a desolation…[and] shall serve the king of Babylon seventy years,* (Jer.25:11), a prophecy fulfilled by Nebuchadnezzar's conquest of Jerusalem; or in Isaiah's prophecy against the northern Israelite kingdom of Ephraim, *and within threescore and five years shall Ephraim be broken, that it be not a people,* (Isaiah 7:8), a prophecy fulfilled with the Assyrian conquest and eradication of Ephraim in 723 B.C. Both prophecies are a straight count of years, warning and punishment.

(iii) the principle of a day for a year, validated by two witnesses: Thus, in Numbers, the Israelites are punished for sinning with the golden calf while Moses was on Mount Sinai for forty days, *And your children shall wander in the wilderness forty years… After the number of the days in which ye searched the land, even forty days, each day for a year, shall ye bear your iniquities, even forty years,* (Num.14:33-34). And again, in Ezekiel, *And thou shalt bear the iniquity of the house of Judah forty days: I have appointed thee each day for a year,* (Eze.4:6). The day for a year principle is the one commonly applied in most prophecy readings which involve a precise count of days in fulfilment of the prophecy. These prophecies may also use the stopwatch principle discussed earlier; most notable in this class of prophecy is the Seventy Weeks of Daniel, still unfolding.

(iv) the principle of one day as a thousand years, also validated by two witnesses: *Be not ignorant of this one thing, that one day is with the Lord as a thousand years, and a thousand years as one day,* (2 Peter 3:8); and again, *For a thousand years in thy sight are but as yesterday when it is past,* (Psalm 90:4). The day as a thousand years applies in sweeping timespans; as in the six days of creation, where six equals the six thousand years allotted to man, followed by a day of rest, the millennial kingdom of God. This 'sweep of time' principle clarifies God's pronouncement, *My spirit shall not always strive with man for that he also is flesh: yet his days shall be an hundred and twenty years,* (Gen.3:6). Man's mortal allotment is six thousand years; the unambiguous translation is then one hundred twenty *jubilee* years = six thousand years, followed by a suggestion of judgement 'shall not strive.' The idea of jubilee or fifty years is a repeated time division in the Bible, a conclusion to seven sevens, the smaller time block.

Prophecy is God's way of communicating with his people. He warns and advises through the prophets who speak his holy word –

Surely the LORD GOD will do nothing, but he revealeth his secret unto his servants the prophets, (Amos 3:7).

The straight timelines are most frequently a near judgement, warned and then carried out; as the forty-year punishment in the wilderness, the Babylonian captivity or Ephraim's destruction.

The convoluted timelines offer the student a chance at grace or awareness, for the preservation of his/her soul. Thus the Seventy-Weeks Prophecy delivered by Gabriel (which we will study next) lays out a timeline to the first coming of Jesus Christ and also to his second coming. The third and fourth visions of Daniel carry numbers and precise incidents, including geography, and are directly linked to unlocking Revelation for that same purpose, that the student of his word may recognise these events which will come cloaked in deception and images of peace, and recognising them may preserve his soul.

God lays out his word for us to understand.

Proverbs encourages us to seek understanding, *It is the glory of God to conceal a thing: but the honour of kings is to search out a matter,* (Prb.25:2).

The Apostle Peter warns, *Knowing this first, that no prophecy of the scripture is of private interpretation,* (2 Peter 1:20).

Right understanding is done in humility –
Thus saith the LORD, Let not the wise man glory

in his wisdom, neither let the mighty man glory in his might... but let him that glorieth glory in this, that he understandeth and knoweth me, that I am the LORD, (Jer.9:23-24).

Let us return to Daniel's visions. As often happens in sequential prophecy, each subsequent prophecy expands on the last. Two years after his second vision, Daniel receives another (in the third year of King Belshazzar). He is resting by the river Ulai in Elam (a region in the southwest of modern Iran, partly in Iraq), when he sees a ram standing on the bank of the river. The ram has one horn higher than the other; it pushes westward, northward and southward so strongly that no animal can resist it. Suddenly, from the west, comes a goat with a single large horn, travelling so swiftly that its feet do not touch the ground; the goat rushes at the ram; the goat breaks the ram's horns and tramples the ram underfoot. Then the goat's large horn suddenly snaps off and in its place grow four horns, *And out of one of them came forth a little horn,* (ch.8:9).

Here we meet the little horn for a second time. He is busy carrying out his agenda:

- he waxes great, even to the host of heaven
- the place of the sanctuary is cast down
- the daily sacrifice is taken away

- he casts truth to the ground
- he practises and prospers

Daniel is still contemplating the vision when a powerful figure appears, so mighty that Daniel falls to the ground. This powerful angel lifts Daniel up. He identifies himself as the angel Gabriel and informs Daniel that the vision is not for the present, but *at the time of the end shall be the vision* (ch.8:17).

Gabriel proceeds to explain the vision. This time the empires are named and the future is laid bare in three short sentences: *The ram which thou sawest having two horns are the kings of Media and Persia. And the rough goat is the king of Greecia: and the great horn that is between the eyes is the first king. Now that being broken, whereas four stood up for it, four kingdoms shall stand up out of the nation,* (ch.8:20-22).

The prophecy in this vision is so precise that sceptics claim these words were added into the Book of Daniel at a much later date, after Alexander's conquest, death and the division of his empire (remember, the vision is during the Babylonian empire). It is worth noting here that Daniel's writings appear in the apocrypha of the Septuagint, started in the third century B.C. and completed in 132 B.C.; fragments of the Book of Daniel, accurate with later transcripts, appear in the Dead Sea Scrolls of Qum'ran authenticating its provenance to this period, if not earlier. Sceptics who insist on later-date-additions to Daniel are unable to explain why the chain of empires do not go beyond a fourth; they cannot explain the forecasted division of the last empire into its eastern and western legs, clearly well into the future (Constantinople was founded in 330 A.D.); they cannot explain the knowledge that this empire never 'dies,' merely amalgamates into ordinary life (the feet of iron and clay); nor can these sceptics explain the Seventy-Weeks Prophecy which follows, still playing out over two thousand years later, in our modern world.

Instead, let us accept the visions as revealed, and the explanations as stated.

The animals of the third vision draw an easy parallel with their counterparts in the last: the uneven horns of the ram a reminder of the hunched bear, the goat's feet which do not touch the ground matching the leopard. The push of the ram west, north and south position the three major conquests of Medo-Persia: Lidia (Turkey), Babylon (Iran-Iraq) and Egypt; the goat's approach from the west marks Greece's geographical position vis-à-vis the Medo-Persian empire; Alexander's victories at Granicus, Issus and Gaugamela (a triumph of military strategy still studied by war historians today) represent the ram being stomped upon. Persian power is broken, Darius III flees. Then the goat's horn abruptly snaps off. It tells of Alexander's sudden death by fever and the carving up of his sprawling kingdom by his four generals, represented by the four horns which replace the single horn, growing in four different directions.

From one of these horns grows a little horn.

This is our second prophetic view of the antichrist; but the first offering of a tangible which can be tracked: the antichrist will arise from one of these four kingdoms of the divided Greek empire or be a descendant of this region (figure xii).

Qualities of the antichrist are repeated: he lies, he boasts, he prospers.

Two specific actions are added: he defiles the sanctuary and takes away the daily sacrifice. Daniel hears two angels discuss a *transgression of desolation*, (ch.8:13; biblically, desolation or abomination refer to idol worship) which defiles the sanctuary (a holy place, not necessarily a temple). A time span is laid out by the angels for this period desolation, 2300 days.

Let us examine this number –

2300 days = 6.3 years, approx. 6yrs, 4mths.

This period, delivered by the angels, has confirmed the belief that it aligns with a slightly abbreviated seven-year tribulation period (*and except those days should be shortened, there should no flesh be saved,* Matt. 24:22), with three and a half years belonging within it as the great tribulation.

Interestingly, if we look at this prophecy using the prophetic principle of one day for a year, we are carried back from our present era to that very period

92 | END ZONE

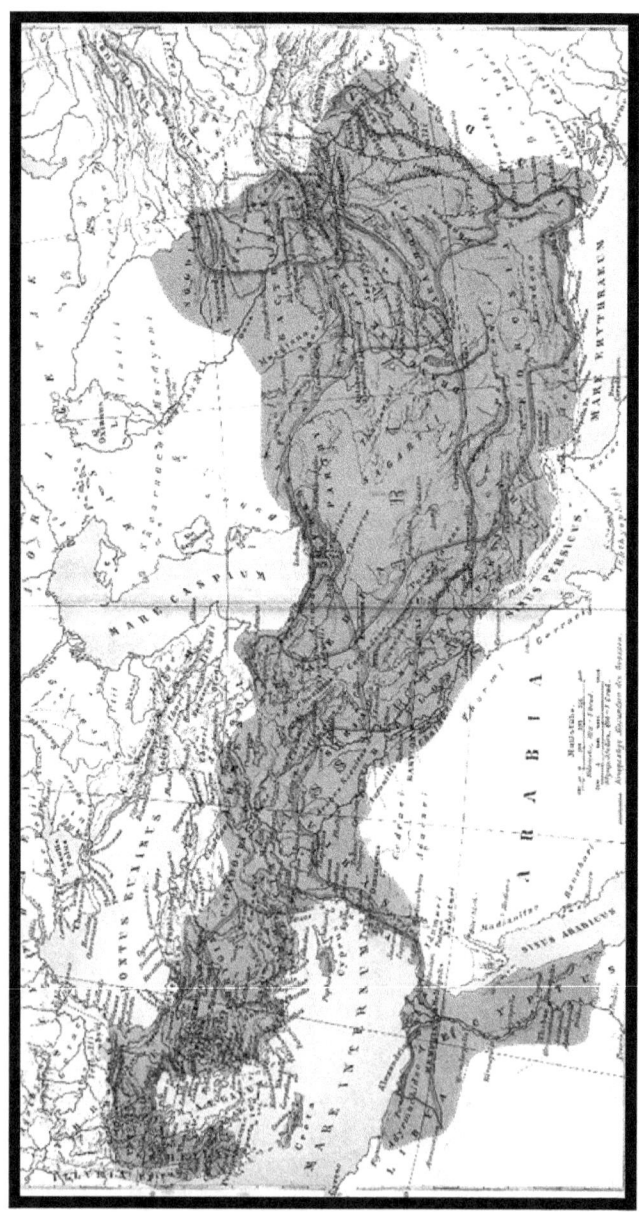

Fig. xii: Map showing extent of the Empire of Alexander the Great at his death in 332 B.C., conquests shown with Latin nomenclature, published in Germany in 1893

with which the prophecy deals, the divided empire of Alexander the Great.

Following Alexander's sudden death in 332 B.C., his empire was held in regency for his baby son Alexander IV; but as the boy entered his teens he was murdered by order of Cassander and the empire was carved up between his four governing generals: Seleucus, Ptolemy, Cassander and Lysimachus.

Seleucus, satrap over the large northeastern region, declared kingship in 305 B.C; Ptolemy, who controlled the southern region of Egypt and the Sinai, followed suit.

There were continuous battles between the Ptolemaic and Seleucid dynasties following the drawing of these borders. In 301 B.C., Ptolemy I aggressed against his Seleucid neighbour, seeking control over a dividing swath of land between the two empires, including the area in which Jerusalem lay. The belief of the Jewish people was corrupted by Greek pantheism. A major defilement of the temple occurred in 167 B.C., when the Seleucid king Antiochus IV Epiphanes (phonetic similarity to antichrist?), set up a statue of Zeus in the Second Temple and famously slaughtered a pig on the altar, commanding that its flesh be eaten by all to show submission to Greek gods. The high priest who had been chosen by the Seleucid king was complicit with the action and a majority of Jews accepted the sacrilege; but a rural rabbi Mattathias, in the village of Modi'in, refused the orders of the Seleucid officials in 166 B.C.; he and his five sons (including Judas 'Maccabee,' so nicknamed for his hammer/guerilla strikes against the Seleucids), led the Maccabean revolt. They were slowly joined by others. The revolt lasted seven years ending in the cleansing of the temple and the institution of a new feast, Hanukkah.

The temple desecration and the actions of Antiochus IV Epiphanes are symbolically significant, providing a historical template for the antichrist and the final days. The triumph of a small, vastly outnumbered group of men, the Maccabees, is also symbolically significant.

Rich prophecies often hold dual chronology, a foreshadowing and subsequent 'true' fulfilment (as in Passover and Christ's crucifixion; as in the virgin birth and the Rev.12 sign), though the 'true' events, when they occur, present in very different ways.

The third vision adds depth to the antichrist profile:

- he will be a king (leader) of fierce countenance
- he will understand dark sentences (the occult)
- he will be mighty but not by his own power (receive outside [?] support)
- he will come in peace but destroy many
- he will be broken without hand (supernaturally)

The phrase 'broken without hand' recalls the stone which smote the statue in the king's dream.

The stone, of course, is Jesus.

This image of a stone appears repeatedly in the Old and New Testament, *The stone which the builders rejected, the same is become the head of the corner: this is the Lord's doing and it is marvellous in our eyes* (Matt.21:42; Luke 20:17-18; Mark 12:10); he is the *chief cornerstone* (Eph.2:20); and again, *the stone which was set at naught of you builders, which is become the head of the corner* (Acts 4:11; Psalm 118:22); and yet again, *And he shall be for a sanctuary; but for a stone of stumbling and for a rock of offence to both the houses of Israel, for a gin and for a snare to the inhabitants of Jerusalem. And many among them shall stumble and fall, and be broken, and be snared, and be taken*, (Isaiah 8:14-15).

Gabriel concludes by instructing Daniel to 'shut up the vision' for it belongs to the end of time. But it is a dark picture which precedes the deliverance of God.

Daniel writes, *And I Daniel fainted, and was sick certain days…*

Daniel's final vision does not involve statues or animals but is rather an angelic encounter and the unveiling of a plot. It takes place towards the end of Daniel's life. The Babylonian empire has fallen and Cyrus the Great is on the throne of Persia; it is the third year of his reign. The Jews are freed from bondage but Daniel continues in the service of the king as a high government official and he continues to be faithful to the word of God.

Chapter 10 begins with mention of a three-week fast which Daniel has just completed. He is walking by the river with friends when a powerful figure clothed in fine linen, with eyes like fire, limbs the colour of molten brass and a voice as that of a multitude appears before him. Daniel falls to the ground and his friends who do not see the vision are overcome with fear and flee. The angel lifts Daniel up and reassures him, *O Daniel, a man greatly beloved, understand the words that I speak unto thee, and stand upright: for unto thee I am now sent,* (ch.10:11).

It is the angel Gabriel. He brings an account of the last days for Daniel to write down but he starts with a strange story about 'the prince of Persia' who held him back for twenty-one days, till the archangel Michael helped Gabriel break free.

[N.B. The 'prince of Persia' is a euphemism for Satan, similar to Ezekiel's 'king of Tyrus' and 'pharaoh, king of Egypt' (Eze.28:11-19, 31:2-14) where the correlation is more clearly made.]

It is a curious tale with no parallels in the Bible.

This prologue to Gabriel's account of the last days highlights a spiritual struggle also scheduled to play out in the last days, a bitter attempt to suppress the truth told in physical terms, a rubber-meets-the-road event.

Gabriel then begins his message.

He once again predicts the end of Persian power (at the time of this final vision Persian power has just begun) and the rise of a powerful king from Greece whose kingdom shall be divided by four men. The chief players of the end-time plot will arise from this divided Greek empire, for *out of a branch of her roots shall one stand up in his estate,* (ch.11:7); *a mighty king shall stand up, that shall rule with great dominion, and do according to his will,* (ch.11:3).

The 'branch of her roots' offers some ambiguity.

The final drama will play out in the Middle East but will the start of the plot lie elsewhere? The suggestion seems to be of a descendant from this area rather than the area itself.

The plot that unfolds revolves around the king of the north and the king of the south. The story is of broken treaties, a disrespected daughter and insulted envoys (ch.11:6); of aggression, war, defeat and victory; a visit to the glorious land, (ch.11:16, Israel); and another strange alliance in which one king offers the other *the daughter of women, corrupting her, but she shall not stand on his side,* (ch.11:17; it suggests an unsuccessful marriage/treaty; the word 'corruption' opens many possibilities); then this king stumbles and falls (ch.11:19) and is replaced by a raiser of taxes, who is soon *destroyed neither in anger nor in battle,* (ch.11:20, health?), *and in his place shall stand up a vile person,* (ch.11:21).

This 'vile person' is welcomed by many.

A treaty is now signed, *And after the league made with him he shall work deceitfully: for he shall come up, and shall become strong with a small people,* (ch.11:23).

Deceit and pretence are emphasized features in this end-time tale.

Overwhelming deceit is also Christ's warning in the Olivet discourse. Mark's gospel begins Jesus's account of the last days with these words, *Take heed lest any man deceive you,* (Mark 13:5).

To return to Gabriel's saga –

Even while entering into the league/treaty, the vile person works to undermine it; he enters peaceably 'upon the fattest provinces,' (ch.11:24); his power base is 'with a small people,' i.e. his popularity is with the 'small' people of the world or the masses; alternately his power is through a small group of people, the elite. Following the league/treaty, this king returns to his own land with great riches (ch.11:28), but his heart shall be against God's law (ch.11:28) and he returns to have intelligence *with them that forsake the holy covenant,* (ch.11:30).

Meanwhile continuous and confused movement continues between the king of the north and the king of the south, *And both these king's hearts shall be to do mischief, and they shall speak lies at one table, but it shall not prosper: for yet the time shall be at the time appointed,* (ch.11:27). The 'appointed time' is reached when the 'daily sacrifice' is taken away; and *they shall place the abomination that maketh desolate,* (ch.11:31).

These words are in the Seventy-Weeks Prophecy.

These words are spoken by Jesus in the Olivet discourse, (Matt.24:15).

These words are a re-statement of the actions of the little horn of chapter 8.

Gabriel now attaches some qualities to the king of the verse of 11:36, all of which match the little horn. He shall –

- do according to his will
- exalt and magnify himself above every god
- speak marvellous things against the God of gods
- not regard the God of his fathers
- not regard the desire of women (?)
- honour the god of forces (war, violence)
- increase with glory a strange god (?)
- divide the land for gain
- prosper till the indignation be accomplished

An overwhelming number of these pointers highlight false worship.

False worship is central to the end-times battle.

False worship is the sole – at first camouflaged

goal – of the antichrist.

Pointers to this king include the 'new' worship of a 'strange' god who is worshipped in 'the most strongholds' (great privacy) and given great glory (ch.11:39); *a god whom his fathers knew not,* (ch.11:38). The emphasized strangeness of this god implies something very extraordinary – even extra-terrestrial? Does it link to the alien saviour agenda postulated by prophecy writers like Thomas Horn and Chris Putnam?

This antichrist/king worships a 'god of fortresses' and his success in battle is linked to 'devices' (ch.11:24, 25). The nature of these devices is not explained but they foreshadow the military power of the beast of Revelation, *Who is like unto the beast? who is able to make war with him?* (Rev.13:4).

Who is this man?

Is he the king of the north... or south?

Reading through the twisting plot of intrigue with the repeated use of 'he,' moving from one to the other without clarity, it is difficult to make a categorical statement. The action seems to favour the king of the north; the phrase, however, *out of a branch of her roots* is clearly the king of the south.

Let us turn to history for guidance – because though the conclusion of Gabriel's story is clearly stated as end-time future (ch.12:9), yet history informs us that much of the plot has already played out in the past between the Ptolemaic and Seleucid dynasties, between 300-160 B.C. The prophecy is clearly one of dual fulfilment.

Historically, Ptolemy I aggressed against the Seleucid king in 301 B.C., occupying Coele-Syria (now Lebanon); when beaten back, Ptolemy II offered his daughter Bernice in marriage to the Seleucid king Antiochus II, 252 B.C.; Bernice and her son were eventually murdered triggering further war; the other marriage alliance is Antiochus III's daughter Cleopatra (not of Marc Antony fame) to Ptolemy V, 193 B.C., in a (failed) attempt to gain Egypt.

Historically, the Jews welcomed Antiochus III, assisting in his battle against Ptolemy V, c.197 B.C.; it resulted, however, in bitter subjugation under his successor Antiochus IV Epiphanes who looted Jerusalem and sold the office of high priest; Antiochus IV Epiphanes later returned to force compliance with Greek culture, leading to the temple desecration and the slaughtered pig (167 B.C., already discussed).

We are informed through the Olivet discourse and Daniel's Seventy-Weeks Prophecy that another abomination/defilement is tied to end-times. We can therefore expect some variation of the events listed above to play out during the last days, including the confused movement (behind-the-scenes manipulation), high level intrigue and political deceit – not marriages, but in those days marriages were basically treaties; not slaughtered pigs, but an enforcement of the profane.

Historically, Gabriel's revealed plot played out between 300-160 B.C. but we can expect the end-time action to be a time-compressed composite (as the beast of Revelation is a theme-compressed composite of the old empires that form it).

Historically, Antiochus III's foolish foray beyond his western borders into Greece (the empires of Cassander and Lysimachus had already fallen to the Roman Republic) drew the attention of a new and powerful player; Rome would wipe out the Seleucid empire and put the area under their control within the next fifty years.

The king of the north in end-time play is not one individual (nation) and his descendants (governments), but the concerted actions of those nations (identified as north or south vis-à-vis their capital's latitude placement to Jerusalem) who entered the Middle East as players during the U.S./coalition search for non-existent WMDs. These 'kings' return to their countries with the 'riches' of war (oil, gas, construction contracts); they find common ground with others who are 'against the holy covenant' and return to plot with them. Gabriel's story suggests a concerted effort against the laws of God by a group of nations.

Gradually one man emerges as supreme.

The antichrist.

Historically, the Jews welcomed Antiochus III

(leading to their downfall). Why? Because Antiochus was fighting Ptolemy/Egypt, the enemy of Israel, who had overrun their country to reach his goal Coele-Syria.

Will something similar play out in the last days? Will the wars fought against Israel's traditional enemies trap them into a false choice? Chris White in his book, *False Christ*, highlights the dual nature of the awaited Jewish messiah presented through Moshiach ben Yosef and Moshiach ben David: are they, in fact, different men?

Sorting through the convoluted plot of conflict and deceit, the final indication for the antichrist appears to lie with the king of the north, i.e. the Seleucid dynasty (certainly the Seleucid king Antiochus IV Epiphanes put in place the abomination of desolation). The old Seleucid empire comprised an immense sweep of land in an uneven band across modern Turkey, Syria, Lebanon, Iraq, Iran, Kuwait, Afghanistan and Pakistan; the empire's northern borders touched parts of modern Armenia, Azerbaijan, Turkmenistan, Tajikistan, Uzbekistan with a narrow arm stretching upwards into Kazakhstan and Kyrgyzstan.

The placing of the 'abomination' sets the final scene, the great tribulation. The antichrist will *plant the tabernacles of his palace between the seas in the glorious holy mountain,* (ch.11:45); the 'holy mountain' suggests Mount Moriah which lies between the Mediterranean

Sea and Dead Sea.

The emergent antichrist does not initiate the final round of battle, however. That action comes from the king of the south. In the divided Greek empire it was an area ruled by Ptolemy, comprising Egypt and parts of Libya, Sudan and Ethiopia.

Interestingly, the prophecy of Ezekiel, chapter 38, indicates these same geographical areas in an end-time war (figure xiii). Ezekiel's list of combatants reads, *Gog, the chief prince of Meshech and Tubal… Persia, Ethiopia and Libya with them…Gomer, and all his bands; the house of Togarmah of the north quarters, and all his bands,* (Eze.38:3-6).

Meshech (Asia Minor/Turkey) and Tubal (Syria) are named as principalities of Gog, ruler of Magog, a Japhetite tribe, identified by the historian Flavius Josephus with Cappadocia (modern Turkey); in Ezekiel's time, there was also a city in Cappadocia called Tagarma, directly north of Israel. Some Bible scholars place Gomer as the area around the Black Sea, and Magog as the region between the Black Sea and the Caspian Sea. Other indications are clear: Persia is modern Iran-Iraq; Ethiopia (also called Cush, a loosely structured area that includes portions of modern Sudan and southern Egypt) and Libya (also called Phut).

As with any war there are participants and spectators. Sheba and Dedan, ancient cities of Saudi Arabia are mentioned as spectators of the war, together

DANIEL, THE VISIONS | 105

Fig. xiii: Ezekiel 38; this 1854 map locates Meshech together with Gog and Magog, roughly in the southern Caucasus.

with Tarshish (not to be confused with Tarsus in south Turkey, birthplace of the Apostle Paul), an uncertain region, sometimes cited as a sea trader with Israel and Phoenicia.

Ezekiel's mention of Tarshish is a curious one –

It reads, *Sheba, and Dedan, and the merchants of Tarshish, with all the young lions thereof, shall say unto thee, Art thou come to take a spoil? hast thou gathered thy company to take a prey?* (Eze.38:13).

Tarshish has been linked to Britain in prophetic interpretation, a merchant sea-faring nation carrying the lion on its coat of arms; the 'young lions' are seen as Britain's ex-colonies, the U.S. and Commonwealth nations, who will question the war; the suggestion is that these far-flung countries join with Saudi Arabia in protesting it. Ezekiel 38 is widely seen as predicting an end-time gathering of nations against Israel, though not the actual battle of Armageddon.

[N.B. An alternate view places the Gog-Magog war as occurring post-Armageddon (Jewish scholars tend to place it with Messiah Ben-David), in a time of complete security and unwalled cities; in this case it will match the end of the millennial kingdom when Satan is set loose 'a little while' (Rev.20:7-8), in a failed final attempt against the people and city of God; if Ezekiel 38 plays out in our time, it will be a foreshadowing of that ultimate future fulfillment.]

Returning to a current day interpretation of the

old Seleucid empire, scholars like Dr. J. Paul Tanner (essay, *Daniel's King of the North*, 1992) propose a last-days northern Arab confederation to be hermeneutically consistent with Daniel's text; others favour Turkey or Iran, both key players in the region; yet others favour Russia because the northern reaches of the Seleucid empire included part of old U.S.S.R., a theory especially popular during Cold War geopolitics (now, with current tension, becoming popular again). However modern Russia does not lie within the old Seleucid empire; Russia's role can only be by proxy or subsequent to the initial conflict, perhaps entering battle when 'the young lions' do. It is even possible that Russia, still associated with the hammer symbol, will represent the action of the Maccabees (Hebrew for 'hammer'). It will be remembered that the Maccabees singlehandedly challenged the action of Antiochus IV Epiphanes in his desecration of the Temple, (leading to revolt and victory, and ending with Hanukkah).

Prophecy, as seen, may hold layers of fulfillment.

The final push is into the 'glorious land,' (ch.11:41). This push links to a time referred to as Jacob's Trouble, spoken of in Isaiah, *when the glory of Jacob shall be made thin, and the fatness of his flesh shall wax lean*, (Isaiah 17:4).

Significantly, this prophecy in Isaiah closely follows a prophecy on Damascus: *Behold, Damascus is taken away from being a city, and it shall be a ruinous heap*, (Isaiah 17:1). Damascus, the capital of Syria, is distinguished in history as a city with continuous and unbroken habitation stretching back five thousand plus years, one of a small handful of cities which may claim the distinction of continuous settlement. But today Damascus is more rubble than city, the consequence of a vicious civil war which grew from the Arab Spring of 2011, fueled by external players and funded by those on both sides of the political spectrum. The images from this war zone show a destroyed and ravaged city, its veneer of civilization largely stripped away. Prophecy scholars believe that the prerequisite condition for Jacob's Trouble has been met.

Noteworthy, in this clash of nations, are three ancient kingdoms which escape carnage: Edom, Moab and Ammon (ch.11:41).

These areas all lie in modern Jordan.

The war against Israel escalates into *a time of trouble, such as never was since there was a nation even to that same time: and at that time thy people shall be delivered, every one that shall be found written in the book*, (ch.12:1). The archangel Michael is referenced as this agent of deliverance; he descends to join the battle below. Though not stated as such, this event fits the Second Coming of Christ and his heavenly host, detailed in the Book of Revelation.

The dead are awakened, *some to everlasting life and some to shame*, (ch.12:3).

Daniel is told, *But thou, O Daniel, shut up the words, and seal the book, even to the time of the end* (ch.12:4). And once again a timeline is laid out, *And from the time that the daily sacrifice shall be taken away, and the abomination that maketh desolate set up, there shall be a thousand two hundred and ninety days. Blessed is he that waiteth and cometh to the thousand three hundred and five and thirty days,* (ch.12:11-12).

A period of great tribulation followed by blessing.

Three and a half years (plus), we came across that number before.

5 – the Seventy-Weeks Prophecy

Hindsight is 20/20. This is the triumph of validating prophecy, the complexity of living it; of attempting to decipher an event, of sorting through a barrage of astounding news and then realising that some quiet incident which slipped by with little fanfare is assuming unexpected significance.

As this is today's difficulty, so was it a difficulty in the past.

Prophecy in the past was further confused by conflicting empires vying for power, of uncertain and shifting borders and historical records tied to the reign of each king. Thus King Astyages of the Medes (585-550 B.C.) ruled simultaneously with the (at first weaker) alliance partner King Cambyses I of Persia (580-559 B.C.); in this way the tenth year of Astyages of the Medo-Persians and the fifth year of Cambyses, also of the Medo-Persians, mean the same year, 575 B.C. Timelines get further muddied when rivals fight for power and the start of a reign is not clear till history proves it as such. The Medo-Persian empire only consolidated under Cyrus II, also known as Cyrus the Great (559-530 B.C.), son of Cambyses I, and grandson of Astyages through his daughter Mandane.

It should be noted that the Old Testament writings record events strictly as they relate to Israel; thus the decree in the Book of Ezra which is stated as occurring in *the first year of Cyrus king of Persia* (Ezra 1:1) is not the year 559 B.C. when Cyrus took the Persian throne, but the year Cyrus conquered Babylon where the Jews were held captive, gaining control of their future, i.e. 539 B.C.

It may also be noted that one of the most astounding Bible prophecies is found in Isaiah, when Cyrus is mentioned nearly 150 years before his birth: God calls him by name, *That saith of Cyrus, He is my shepherd, and shall perform all my pleasure: even saying to Jerusalem, Thou shalt be built; and to the temple, Thy foundation shall be laid* (Isaiah 44:28); and again, *Thus saith the LORD to his anointed, to Cyrus, whose right hand I have holden… I, the LORD, which call thee by thy name, am the God of Israel,* (Isaiah 45:1-3).

It is also worth noting (for the sake of order) that chapters 5 and 6 in the book of Daniel are not sequential; they should follow chapter 9. It would seem that Daniel wrote his visions and defining events on separate parchment rolls which were later placed together, (including a chapter by

Nebuchadnezzar himself).

Thus, in chapter 9, Daniel is found counting the prophesized years of captivity, believing them near completion; but, in chapter 5, Belshazzar of Babylon is already overthrown following his mighty feast. Extra biblical texts state that Belshazzar had likewise counted the years of captivity, arrived at seventy years, and decided that the God of the Israelites had forgotten them and/or was not to be feared. Belshazzar calls for the temple vessels from Jerusalem and uses them in a boastful drunken orgy; and *in that same hour came forth fingers of a man's hand and wrote… upon the plaister of the wall of the king's palace [and] the king's countenance was changed,* (ch.5:5-6). The words were 'Mene Mene Tekel Upharsin' which translated means, God hath numbered thy kingdom and finished it.

Daniel writes, *In that night was Belshazzar the king of the Chaldeans slain. And Darius the Median took the kingdom, being about threescore and two years old,* (ch.5:30-31).

[N.B. Mene Mene Tekel Upharsin are verbs and also weights/coins: thus mene=1000 gerahs, mene=1000 gerahs, tekel= 20 gerahs, upharsin= 500 gerahs, totalling 2520 gerahs.

2520 appears to be associated with judgement.

2520 days (7 years x 360 biblical days) is the length of the king's madness (following Nebuchadnezzar's statue of gold before which all must worship).

A seven-year tribulation is also 2520 days; the Book of Revelation confirms a three-and-a-half year reign of antichrist but the missing week of Daniel (i.e. the seventieth week, 7 years) suggests a possible three-and-a-half year 'build up.']

The mention of Darius is a strange one. History does not record such a man till Darius I, twenty years later; yet Daniel references Darius the Mede two more times, in both cases setting a timeframe for the chapter. Darius is carefully recorded as *the son of Ahasuerus, of the seed of the Medes, which was made king over the realm of the Chaldeans*, (ch.9:1).

Perhaps the best explanation lies in the man's age, an unusual inclusion since he was no minor. Darius appears to be a cousin of Cyrus, about the same age as Cyrus (there is no birth date for Cyrus, his birth is placed between 600/576 B.C.). Victory and kingship lay with Cyrus the Persian who captured Babylon; but as Cyrus continued in battle subjugating resistance within the Babylonian kingdom and moving towards Egypt (eventually conquered by his son Cambyses II), Cyrus could easily have left his friend and cousin in charge of the fallen city, hence the phrase 'was made king over' instead of 'became.'

This also explains the start of chapter 9, *In the first year of Darius*; the first year of Darius (standing in for Cyrus) is also the last year of Belshazzar (described in chapter 5), and explains Daniel's activity of counting the years of captivity. It shows the immediacy of Daniel's writing, given that (till Cyrus), the Medes and the Persians both held the position of kings. The innocent and understandable error unintentionally authenticates the Book of Daniel as being written at the time claimed; such an error would not have occurred later, indeed it is corrected by Daniel himself. Daniel's realisation of the actual order of government is made apparent in chapter 10 when he writes, *In the third year of Cyrus king of Persia* (ch.10:1); this opens his final vision.

With this background, let us turn to the Seventy-Weeks Prophecy of Daniel which is at the forefront of all prophecy study today.

It belongs to chapter 9 of the Book of Daniel.

The year is 539 B.C.

Daniel is at prayer. He was a young man when he rose to prominence with the king's dream; he has enjoyed many years of high service in the Babylonian empire; he is now in his late seventies, possibly eighty. He has been reading the prophet Jeremiah who prophesized the Babylonian captivity and its allotted span of seventy years, and Daniel realises that they are close to the end of this period. He is on his knees petitioning God for mercy, for himself and the other Israelites still in captivity.

While he is praying, the angel Gabriel appears.

Gabriel has a message which he has been commanded to deliver to Daniel: a timeline to the Messiah and to the last days. It is not a vision but a prophecy.

The prophecy is in four verses, as follows:

^{24}Seventy weeks are determined upon thy people and upon the holy city, to finish the transgression and to make an end of sins, and to make reconciliation for iniquity, and to bring in everlasting righteousness, and to seal up the vision and prophecy, and to anoint the most Holy.

^{25}Know therefore and understand, that from the going forth of the commandment to restore and to rebuild Jerusalem unto the Messiah the Prince shall be seven weeks, and threescore and two weeks: the street shall be built again, and the wall, even in troublous times.

^{26}And after threescore and two weeks shall Messiah be cut off, but not for himself: and the people of the prince that shall come shall destroy the city and the sanctuary; and the end thereof shall be with a flood, and unto the end of the war desolations are determined.

^{27}And he shall confirm the covenant with many for one week: and in the midst of the week he shall cause the sacrifice and oblation to cease, and for the overspreading of abominations he shall make it desolate, even until the consummation, and that determined shall be poured upon the desolate (ch.9:24-27).

We will start with the first verse which lays out a timeline and the component parts of the prophecy, *Seventy weeks are determined upon thy people* –

Seventy weeks = 490 days

Clearly 490 days did not bring everlasting righteousness in Daniel's time; we do not have everlasting righteousness even today. Even more clear, the Messiah did not show up in Daniel's time. A safe conclusion? – the interpretation of a straight timeline does not work.

We move then to the alternate timespan, a day for a year.

490 days = 490 years

The first verse therefore states that 490 years are granted to the Jewish people and to Jerusalem to 'finish the transgression,' 'make an end of sin,' 'make reconciliation for iniquity.' All three phrases carry the same meaning of atonement for sin. Repeated thrice suggests a grievous sin has been committed and must be atoned for; proper atonement will bring everlasting righteousness.

Atonement and consequent righteousness will 'seal' the prophecy; here the word 'seal' is not closing up a prophecy for the future but in the sense of fulfilling or satisfying the prophecy.

The final prophetic condition is an anointing of the most Holy.

How will these conditions be met? Verse two, *Know therefore and understand* –

Two sets of numbers appear in this verse:

Seven weeks (7x7=49 years)

Threescore and two weeks (62x7=434 years)

There is no other prophetic rendering in the Bible which divides a single set of numbers into two separate groups, then expects the reader to add them together again to convey the sense of the prophecy. It would seem, then, that the two periods are to be held apart. The timeclock for each period is 'the going forth of the command to restore and rebuild Jerusalem unto the Messiah' – that is to say, after each period of rebuilding, the Messiah is expected. The rebuilding is described as including a 'street' and a 'wall.'

49 biblical years = 48.3 solar years

434 biblical years = 427.8 solar years

Bible scholars have struggled in the interpretation of this verse and their difficulty is compounded by three separate decrees issued by three Medo-Persian kings; not successive kings, but kings separated in their succession to the throne by the intervening reigns of other Persian kings.

Let us look at these kings and their decrees.

Remember the prophecy from Isaiah? – that Cyrus would perform the Lord's pleasure, *even saying to Jerusalem, Thou shalt be built; and to the temple, Thy foundation shall be laid,* (Isaiah 44:28).

History records that Cyrus did indeed free the Jewish captives in Babylon, instructing them to return to their place of origin; a very unusual decree for that period in history where conquest meant enslavement. In addition, Cyrus offered funds from his treasury for rebuilding the Jewish temple. The command of Cyrus is recorded in the Bible, *Now in the first year of Cyrus king of Persia, that the word of the LORD by the mouth of Jeremiah might be fulfilled, the LORD stirred up the spirit of Cyrus king of Persia, that he made a proclamation through all his kingdom, and put it also in writing, saying, Thus saith Cyrus king of Persia, The LORD God of heaven hath given me all the kingdoms of the earth; and he hath charged me to build him an house at Jerusalem, which is in Judah*, (Ezra 1:1-2; also 5:13-15).

The Jews returned to Jerusalem but they met opposition in rebuilding the temple from local authorities; not early in the rebuilding, but later. After struggling for many years with local officials, they finally wrote in complaint to Darius I (522-486 B.C.), now king of Persia. The Bible notes that Darius first verified Cyrus's decree, then issued his own, writing to his officials in the region, *Let the work of this house of God alone…Moreover I make a decree what ye shall do [for] the building of this house of God: that of the king's goods, even of the tribute beyond the river, forthwith expenses be given unto these men, that they be not hindered*, (Ezra 6:7-8).

Which decree should the prophecy count from?

Neither. Both these decrees concern the building of the temple; the 70-week prophecy is tied to the building of Jerusalem with streets and a wall.

The building of Jerusalem appears in the Book of Ezra, chapter 7.

The Book of Ezra opens with a record of Jewish history post-Babylon: Cyrus's decree to rebuild the temple; the names of the men and their households who returned to Jerusalem; the conflicts which caused temple work to cease; the fresh decree from Darius and the completion of the temple in the sixth year of the reign of Darius, (Ezra 6:15).

Ezra's account then moves to himself.

He is a scribe in the palace of Artaxerxes, king of Persia; and he is a priest, a direct descendant of the first priest chosen by God, Moses's brother Aaron (Exo.4:14, 30); seventeenth in line from Aaron. A complete list of Ezra's ancestors follows, tracing his genealogy back to Aaron. This is extremely unusual. The Bible offers a pre- and post-Flood genealogy for the patriarchs in Genesis, one step at a time, as they occur; Matthew offers a detailed genealogy for Jesus Christ, stretching back through three blocks of fourteen generations, forty-two in all (Matt.1:1-17); Luke records a still more detailed genealogy for Christ (Luke 3:23-38); elsewhere, genealogies are reserved for kings and (some) serving high priests (short lists, a few generations at most).

Why this exception for Ezra?

Is he being pointed out?

Ezra writes that in the seventh year of Artaxerxes's reign, he feels the call of God to go to Jerusalem, *and the king granted him all his request, according to the hand of the LORD his God upon him,* (Ezra 7:6). It is not the mere granting of a request but a decree is issued, *Artaxerxes, king of kings, unto Ezra the priest... I make a decree [for Ezra to carry] the silver and gold which the king and his counsellors have freely offered unto the God of Israel, whose habitation is in Jerusalem,* (Ezra 7:12-15).

It is a decree for Jerusalem.

Does this decree start the clock on Daniel's prophecy?

It should. But right away we run into a stumbling block. Artaxerxes I (historically called Artaxerxes Longimanus, meaning 'long hand,' because one arm was longer than the other) reigned from 465-424 B.C. The seventh year of his reign is 458 B.C.

458 B.C. – 427 years = 31 B.C.

Nothing happened, Christ was not yet born.

Unable to come up with a valid reading, Bible scholars attempted adding the two time periods together. What happens if we add both sets of dates to reach 69 weeks, can we get somewhere?

69 weeks = 483 biblical years = 476 solar years

458 B.C. – 476 years = 19 A.D. (adj. for no year 0)

Nothing again; we need a later date or an earlier

date to bring us into a valid time zone for Jesus Christ, his birth or his ministry.

Seeking a solution to this problem, prophecy scholars discovered a passage in the text of Nehemiah, a colleague of Ezra's, a layman who also served in the royal palace as cupbearer to Artaxerxes. The Book of Nehemiah states that in the twentieth year of Artaxerxes, Nehemiah requests permission to visit Judah, *the city of my fathers' sepulchres, that I may build it,* (Neh.2:5). The king asks Nehemiah how long he will be gone (later indicated as about five months in total; the actual work on the wall is stated as fifty-two days, Neh.6:15). Nehemiah requests letters from the king for free passage to Jerusalem and another letter to the king's forester for wood for the wall, which letters are given. Letters for passage and for wood, no decree. But the timing is better. The twentieth year of Artaxerxes's reign (465-424 B.C.) is 445 B.C.

445 B.C. – 427 years = 18 B.C.

No, nothing happened then.

Taking the 69 weeks together, 445 B.C. – 476 years = 32 A.D. (adj. for no year 0)

Much better; it is within the accepted time zone of Jesus Christ. This, they postulate, must be the year Christ died.

But again we run into difficulties.

Is the city rebuilt to the Messiah's coming or his death? Is crucifixion an 'anointing'? More importantly, is it tenable to suppose that a letter, some wood and fifty-two days equate a command to rebuild? Can fifty-two days of work completing (completing, not starting) the walls of Jerusalem be considered as the *going forth of the command to restore and rebuild Jerusalem unto Messiah*?

But if not Nehemiah, what then? – because the Ezra timeline, despite its decree, does not work either. Is there another solution?

Yes, a rather simple one.

There is a later king of that name: Artaxerxes II (historically called Artaxerxes Mnemon, meaning 'whose reign is through truth'), 404-358 B.C.

There is nothing in the Bible that declares Artaxerxes I as the king both Ezra and Nehemiah serve; there is nothing to refute the supposition that it is, in fact, Artaxerxes II Mnemon. The biblical and extra-biblical texts simply place Ezra and Nehemiah together in the reign of an Artaxerxes, nothing more. The birth dates of Ezra and Nehemiah are unknown – why would they be, when even the birth of Cyrus the Great is approximated to within twenty-five years? There is a gap of at least twenty years between the decrees of Cyrus and Darius; there is nothing to deny another eighty years passing before the next decree, the rebuilding of Jerusalem. It is important to note here that though Ezra mentions a completed temple in the sixth year of Darius, he also mentions an Artaxerxes in the rebuilding of the temple in chapter 6 before he starts his personal saga, suggesting that minor work on the temple continued for a while and that an Artaxerxes helped with this effort, *And they builded, and finished it, according to the commandment of the God of Israel, and according to the commandment of Cyrus, and Darius, and Artaxerxes king of Persia,* (Ezra 6:14).

This would be Artaxerxes I, with the temple.

He is part of the historic record of chapters 1-6.

After the historic record, Ezra moves into (his) current time.

The decree to Ezra for Jerusalem, the gold and silver offered for this purpose, the commanded assistance and freedom from levies, the thirteen years that pass in rebuilding before the final wall Nehemiah helps build, Ezra's recorded genealogy as a direct descendant of Aaron – all fall into place if we consider Artaxerxes II. And I submit that even the name Mnemon is an indication of his role, God is careful with the names he gives.

Artaxerxes II ascended the throne in 404 B.C.; *in his seventh year* would be 398 B.C.

398 B.C. – 427 years = 30 A.D. (adj. for no year 0)

30 A.D. places us squarely in the life of Christ.

Is there any specific incident in Christ's life to mark this particular year? We have two dates to work from, his birth and his death. Counting back from the crucifixion date of April 33 A.D. to 30 A.D. gives a period of three years, taking us to an area in time that approximates the start of Christ's ministry. Christ's ministry, the gospels inform us, was immediately preceded by a forty day fast in the wilderness, ending with the temptation by Satan, (Luke 4:1-14; Mark 1:13; Matt.4:1-11).

The fast in the wilderness was immediately preceded by Christ's baptism, (Luke 3:22, 4:1; Mark 1:10-13; Matt. 3:16, 4:1-2).

And we have a biblical text which offers us a date for the baptism: Luke describes the work of John the Baptist as occurring *in the fifteenth year of the reign of Tiberius Caesar*, (Luke 3:1).

The reign of Tiberius Caesar, 14-37 A.D.

His fifteenth year = 29 A.D.

Luke writes about the people who flocked to the River Jordan to be baptised by John; he continues, *Now when all the people were baptised, it came to pass, that Jesus also being baptised, and praying, the heaven was opened. And the Holy Ghost descended… like a dove upon him and a voice came from heaven, which said, Thou art my beloved son; in thee I am well pleased,* (Luke 3:21-22). Matthew's description of the baptism repeats these same elements, including the curious phrase, *the heavens were opened* (Matt.3:16).

[N.B. Bible quotations used are KJV; other respected editions give this same word 'opened' as 'torn open,' 'parting,' 'dividing.']

Once again, as at the birth of Christ, our gaze is directed to the heavens. NASA records a total solar eclipse on November 24, 29 A.D., covering the region of Judaea; occurring just past noon and lasting one minute, fifty-nine seconds.

A supposition: if it had been a cloudy day (unknown), then a solar eclipse with its thermodynamic consequence of a sudden brief cooling of the atmosphere, triggering wind gusts, could have created the visual effect noted by the gospel writers, of clouds rolling apart.

Luke follows the baptism of Jesus Christ with this verse, *And Jesus himself began to be about thirty years of age,* (Luke 3:23). This information validates the 2 B.C. birth of Christ; counting from 2 B.C., Jesus would have attained thirty years in 29 A.D. The information is also significant because, in the Jewish tradition of his time, a man could only assume the title of Rabbi/teacher after reaching the age of thirty.

November 24, 29 A.D., plus a forty day fast in the wilderness, takes us to January 3, 30 A.D. – the start of Christ's ministry, confirming the promise of salvation made to his people long ago; the year fitting perfectly with the end of the sixty-two-week prophetic timeline given by the angel Gabriel to Daniel, marking the first coming.

This date adds to the string of 3s associated with the life of Christ:

- a conception date in 3 B.C.
- Christ's age at baptism, 30 years
- Jan. 3, 30 A.D., Christ's ministry begins in Galilee, a region crossed by the 33rd parallel; he is 30 years old; his ministry will last 3 years and 3 months
- Apr. 3, 33 A.D., Christ's ministry ends; it was the third hour (in the Jewish count of time = 9 a.m.) when they crucified him, Mark 15:25; it is 3 o'clock by the secular count of time (Jewish ninth hour, note the parallelism) when Jesus draws his last breath; he is 33 years old
- the strange 3 which marks Christ's forehead in the image on the shroud.

Is it an emphasis on the Holy Trinity? –

For there are three that bear record in heaven, the Father, the Word, and the Holy Ghost: and these three are one, (1 John 5:7).

The start of 30 A.D. ties loosely into the three-and-a-half time measurement of verse four, *and in the midst of the week* [of years] (ch.9:27), allotting three and a half years to Christ and three and a half to the antichrist (whose time will be shortened, else no flesh would be saved, Matt.24:22); here again is the persistent note of Hebrew parallelism which underlies much prophecy in the Bible and underlines the multi-layered power of this particular prophecy.

The 30 A.D. start-of-Christ's-ministry timeline offers one further validation: it is preceded by the baptism of Christ.

Baptism is an anointing.

It fulfils the criteria of the first verse, *to anoint the most Holy.*

Verse three, *And after threescore and two weeks –*

Here, the required division into two separate time blocks is made abundantly clear. The first span of time is not mentioned, only the second.

The second timespan led to the first coming:

And after threescore and two weeks shall Messiah be cut off, but not for himself: and the people of the prince that shall come shall destroy the city and the sanctuary; and the end thereof shall be with a flood, and unto the end of the war desolations are determined.

The words 'cut off' are used in the Bible to signify death, most often an abruptly shortened lifespan, such as Christ suffered by the crucifixion; the same phrase appears in the Messianic prophecy of Isaiah, *for he was cut off out of the land of the living: for the transgression of my people was he stricken,* (Isaiah 53:8).

'Not for himself' carries a double meaning: Jesus's death was not the result of any crime he had committed; the phrase also indicates that Jesus's death was not for himself but for us, by whose sacrifice we are saved.

The verse carries on with judgement, *the people of the prince that shall come shall destroy the city and the sanctuary.* This section holds prophetic dual fulfilment: remarkably, the Seventy-Weeks Prophecy also plays out on a narrow timeline, seventy weeks as seventy years (figure xiv).

One layer of prophecy played out in 70 A.D. when Jerusalem and the Second Temple were destroyed by the roman army under General Titus Flavius, later to become Caesar, 'the prince that shall come.' Counting seventy years forward from Christ's birth in 2 B.C. brings us to 69 A.D., the end of the permitted period for atonement. The atonement was not made. Judgement fell in 70 A.D. with the destruction of the Second Temple (which put an end to sacrifice) and the destruction of Jerusalem (which led to the Jewish diaspora).

Interesting, in this seventy-year analysis, are the two three-and-a-half-year time spans about the cross: it starts with Christ's ministry; the midpoint is the crucifixion (Jesus Christ, first fruit to God the Father); it closes with the first martyr (St. Stephen, first fruit to Jesus Christ).

Since the Seventy-Weeks Prophecy holds two lines of fulfilment (one for the first coming and one for the second coming), it means that this event will be repeated in some way.

Let us then re-examine the phrase, *the people of*

130 | END ZONE

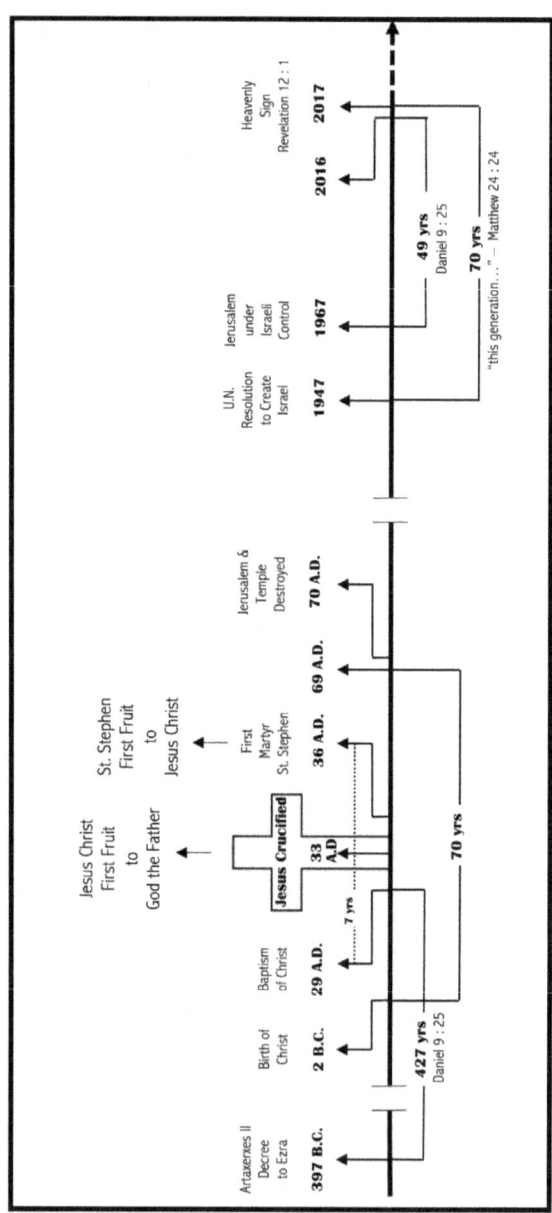

Fig. xiv: Timeline to the First Coming of Jesus Christ; projected timeline for Second Coming

the prince that shall come.

In the judgement that followed the first coming the 'prince' was a roman, General Titus Flavius; the 'people of the prince' were not romans, however, or only in small part. The strategy of the roman army was local conscription under a roman leader. The 'people,' then, are inhabitants of conquered regions close to that area (but not the area itself to prevent fraternity) – in fact the same countries we met in Gabriel's end time account of the king of the north and the south.

Will there be a roman component in the second coming? It seems indicated.

A caveat: in dual fulfilment of prophecy, the event prophesized happens and then happens again, but the trappings will be very different; it will fulfil all elements of the prophecy but in a very different way; the consequences, however, are the same.

What are those consequences? War and desolation, this was the judgement following the unfulfilled period of atonement in the first coming.

And for the second coming?

As we continue the verse, it looks ahead to an event still in the future: *and the end thereof shall be with a flood*. What flood – of water? of blood? Revelation speaks of a flood of water that the dragon pours out after the woman (Rev.12:15); it also mentions a river of blood, *even unto the horse bridles, by the space of a thousand and six hundred furlongs*, (Rev.14:20). In the vial judgements of Revelation, *the sixth angel poured out his vial upon the great river Euphrates; and the water thereof was dried up, that the way of the kings of the east might be prepared,* (Rev.16:12).

The original Greek uses the word 'hodos' for 'way,' meaning a travelled road (*Strong's Concordance* no.G3598); 'road' suggests not simply a drying up, but a catastrophic drying up, such as may be caused by a fissure in the earth or an earth movement in the upper reaches of the river which will result in flooding at the place of breach and consequent dryness in the lower courses of the river. It is a dramatic and observable sign. The 'drying up' of the Euphrates directly precedes Armageddon.

The judgement continues, *And unto the end of the war desolations are determined...*

Verse four, *And he shall confirm the covenant with many for one week: and in the midst of the week he shall cause the sacrifice and oblation to cease, and for the overspreading of abominations he shall make it desolate, even until the consummation, and that determined shall be poured upon the desolate...*

Verse four steps back from the judgement of verse three to the trigger point of these events: a covenant which is confirmed and then broken.

As prophecy watchers see the puzzle pieces come

together in a recognisable but not yet fitted picture, the big question is, which covenant, with whom? All major treaties with a group of signatories (the 'many') have come under scrutiny. Primary among them is the nuclear deal with Iran, July 2015 (now heating up again with Iran's missile test in January 2017 and a threatened re-instatement of sanctions); the Paris Agreement on Climate Change, December 2015 (many signatories, but uncertain how this could impact world events/cause war); and the Paris Peace Summit of January 2017, a joint declaration of nations affirming U.N. Security Council Resolution 2334, supporting a two-state solution for Israel and Palestine, and re-opening a discussion on borders and Jerusalem.

Jerusalem is once again at the forefront of international debate; an epicenter, like a magnet pulling events and nations towards it, fulfilling the prophecy of Zechariah, *Behold, I will make Jerusalem a cup of trembling unto all the people round about… And in that day will I make Jerusalem a burdensome stone for all people: all that burden themselves with it shall be cut in pieces,* (Zech.12:2-3).

The Iran Nuclear Deal and the Paris Peace Summit are, so far (the speed with which world events are moving in fulfilment of prophecy, who can say if a better contender may not yet arise?), the best candidates for 'covenant.' Both agreements are 'with many' and directly affect Israel, though Israel was not present at the table for either deal. Both agreements come in the guise of peace, the breaking of which could cause 'the sacrifice and the oblation to cease.'

Note the word 'confirm' in verse 4, suggesting a pre-existing arrangement.

Does confirmation of the covenant start the daily sacrifice, just as its breaking will end it?

This is the belief of many.

Since the daily sacrifice must first start and then cease, many are convinced that the Third Temple will be soon built. The New Temple description in Ezekiel (chapters 40-43) is sometimes quoted as proof of a third temple – but this text could also match the temple of New Jerusalem, post Armageddon (the measuring reed image certainly matches that of John, in Revelation). However, anticipating a Third Temple in the near future, architectural plans have been drawn up, the holy vessels of the temple have been prepared, the silver trumpets are ready and the Sanhedrin re-convened. In August 2016, a high priest was elected by the Jewish Sanhedrin – for the first time since the destruction of the Second Temple in 70 A.D., almost two thousand years ago.

A broken covenant is also mentioned in the final vision, in Daniel.

I believe there will be a broken covenant and some form of desecration on the temple mount during end times, but it may not be as obvious, and as dramatic, as many think. It may be no more than a multi-faith stele on the Temple Mount, a place declared by God as his own (the site of Abraham's sacrifice, Gen.22:2; and David's sacrifice, 2Chr.3:1), with wording that breaks the First Commandment, *I am the Lord thy God… Thou shalt have no other gods before me,* (Exo.20:2-3; Deut.5:7; Matt.4:10).

In all likelihood the antichrist's broken covenant will directly impact Jerusalem. It is worth recalling that the only example the Bible offers on the wisdom and judgement of Solomon are the quarrelling mothers, the true one and the false one, both claiming the child. The false one agrees to cutting the child in half; the true one relinquishes the child to save its life (1 Kings 3:16-28).

Is this a parable on Jerusalem?

The 'he' of this verse is widely taken to mean the antichrist, an interpretation made popular by Sir Robert Anderson's, *The Coming Prince*. But there is an alternate reading for this prophetic fourth verse when considered in the light of Hebrew parallelism. The 'he' who confirms the covenant with many is Jesus Christ himself; his covenant is with man from the beginning of time. The 'week' would equate seven thousand years (six thousand, Gen.6:3; plus one thousand, Rev.20:5). Christ's crucifixion fell *in the midst of the week*, i.e. at the four-thousand-year mark; it effectively ended sacrifice when the veil of the temple was rent from top to bottom for Jesus was the final sacrifice and the last high priest. The temple was rendered desolate by his death and it will remain so, 'until that determined will be poured upon the desolate.'

This prophetic reading of the fourth verse stands independently, as a layer of prophecy.

It can also overlay the now traditional acceptance of 'he', the antichrist, without denying or detracting from that view; indeed, working with it in an odd contrapuntal harmony, offering depth.

There is one major advantage to this deeper interpretation. Even though the antichrist may break a covenant and install some form of desecration on the temple mount, ending sacrifice in the 'temple' (the temple, in this symbolic read, is ourselves, *Know ye not that ye are the temple of God*, 1Cor.3:16; 1Cor.6:19; John 2:19; those who accept the spiritual defilement of the antichrist are rendered 'desolate'); yet it will not be some huge dramatic event.

It will be quiet, receiving little media coverage.

Low key is an essential part of God's plan.

Low key was a central feature in the first coming of Jesus Christ and it will be equally so in the lead up to his second coming. That last day is to steal up like a thief in the night on those who sleep (Matt.24:43; also Mark 13:35; 1Thess.5:2; 2 Peter 3:10). It is a time of testing but it does not overtly declare itself as such.

The purpose of the end-zone tribulation is to quietly separate the wheat from the chaff.

Did you notice? There was a section in verse two that I did not deal with earlier, a prophetic timeline which belongs to our age, the seven weeks…

Know therefore and understand, that from the going forth of the commandment to restore and to rebuild Jerusalem unto the Messiah the Prince shall be seven weeks, and threescore and two weeks: the street shall be built again, and the wall, even in troublous times.

The two sets of numbers, seven weeks and sixty-two weeks are held apart from each other as separate entities in separate time zones, but they lead up to the same event: the coming of the Messiah.

The second set of numbers led to the first coming; the first set of numbers is, consequently, the lead up to the second coming.

Seven weeks = 49 biblical years = 48.3 solar years

After almost two thousand years of diaspora, Israel is back as a nation and back in the land. The rebirth of Israel took place on May 14, 1948.

[N.B. A little side note, some play of Bible math.

The promise of a nation was first made to Abraham. Using the precise biblical dates set out in Genesis, Abraham appears in the list of patriarchs as being born 1948 years from Adam. Israel took its place among modern nations in 1948.

Between Abraham and Adam, 1948 years.

What happens when we track back 1948 years from Israel's rebirth?

But wait, Daniel informs us that the clock starts from the going forth of the command, i.e. the U.N. Resolution of November, 1947. Tracking back 1948 years from the 'command' date of 1947, and keeping in mind there is no year 0, takes us to 2 B.C., the year of Christ's birth.

Christ is sometimes called the second Adam, for by one man sin came into the world, so by one man it was taken away: *The first man is of the earth, earthy; the second man is the Lord from heaven,* (1Cor.15:47).

Earth and heaven, point and counterpoint.

Like a binding melody in music. Or an equation in math. Or, in scripture, parallelism.]

Returning to Daniel's prophecy –

We have arrived at the rebirth of Israel.

But the prophecy does not deal with Israel, it deals with Jerusalem; the triggering factor is the rebuilding of Jerusalem 'unto the Messiah the Prince'.

In the Six Day War of June 1967, Israel captured East Jerusalem, including the old city and Temple Mount; Bethlehem was also seized.

In 1987 an organised Palestinian resistance began, called the First Intifada. It lasted seven years and ended with the Oslo Accord, 1995: Bethlehem was returned to the jurisdiction of the Palestinian Authority; Israel retained control over Jerusalem but the Al-Aqsa Mosque and the Dome of the Rock, both situated on the Temple Mount, were put under control of the Jordanian-Palestinian Waqf.

In September 2000, the Second Intifada began and the Israeli Knesset responded by commissioning a wall, built along sections of the West Bank, flush with the old city of Jerusalem.

The 'wall' is part of Gabriel's prophecy delivered two thousand, five hundred years ago, the final puzzle piece to fall into place. The wall is part of required prophecy but it does not set the clock ticking: the start of the prophecy is Jerusalem itself, a decree for the city (in this case, war); control of Jerusalem passed to Israel with the Six Day War of 1967.

The year is strongly confirmed –

'We have returned to all that is holy in our land… never to be parted from it again.' [Moshe Dayan, Defense Minister of Israel, June 1967.]

'You have been given the great privilege of returning to the nation its capital and holy center. Jerusalem is yours, forever.' [Commander Mordechai (Motta) Gur to the 55th Paratroopers Brigade, following recapture of the Old City and Temple Mount, June 1967.]

'In the name of the entire Jewish people in Israel and the Diaspora, I hereby recite with supreme joy, Blessed art thou, O Lord our God, King of the universe, who has kept us in life, who has preserved us, and enabled us to reach this day. This year in Jerusalem – rebuilt!' [General Rabbi Shlomo Goren, Chaplain of the Israeli Defense Forces, at the Western Wall, June 1967.]

Jerusalem. Rebuilt.

On June 27, 1967 the Israeli Knesset formally extended Israel's legal and administrative/municipal control to all of Jerusalem.

Thus 1967 + 48.3 = 2015 plus a little, say 2016

2016 ended the period of world grace, to atone for transgression and iniquity.

World grace?

The sixty-two-week timeline announced Christ's ministry to the Jewish people, Jesus made manifest as messiah among his people; it was directed at Israel. The rejection and death of Jesus Christ changed that dynamic – but Jerusalem continues to act as a prophetic timepiece. The seven-week timeline, still tied to Jerusalem, announces the near approach of Christ's Second Coming to the entire world; his crucifixion opened the door of salvation to all who believe in him, *For ye are all the children of God by faith in Jesus Christ... there is neither Jew nor Greek, there is neither bond nor free, there is neither male nor female: for ye are all one in Christ Jesus,* (Gal.3:28).

Remarkably, the years 2015/2016/2017 were indicated as a culminating point by bible scholars writing as far back as the 1700s and 1800s, purely from their study of the Word of God. The private papers of Sir Isaac Newton show that he theorised, in the 1600s, the future re-assembly of Israel as a nation which he saw as a pre-requisite for the end.

The prophecy pieces are in place.

The Second Coming will come quietly.

Amid tribulation, yes. But still a surprise to all except those who watch.

In this reading of prophecy, the 'anointing' is seen either as the heavenly 'birth' sign of Rev.12:1, or alternatively as the Wedding of the Lamb, Rev.19:9, only time will tell.

6 – The Book of Revelation

Grace be unto you, and peace, from him which is, and which was, and which is to come; and from the seven spirits which are before his throne, (Rev.1:4).

Behold, I stand at the door and knock: if any man hear my voice and open the door, I will come in to him and sup with him, and he with me, (Rev.3:20).

The Book of Revelation, sometimes called the Book of the Apocalypse (*apokalypsis*, Greek for revelation), is the central book of Christian eschatology. It is the last book of the Bible and the only book in the Bible which carries a blessing for those who read (or hear) and seek to understand its contents, *Blessed is he that readeth, and they that hear the words of this prophecy, and keep those things which are written therein: for the time is at hand,* (ch.1:3).

Revelation was written by St. John the Divine (popularly identified with the apostle John), about the year 90 A.D.

The book spans three literary genres: epistolary, apocalyptic and narrative. The writing is filled with symbols; it offers a vision of the tribulation period and the day of God's wrath with plot points; it holds a warning and a plea to heed the message of the letters, with which the book starts.

Hefty tomes can be written on this one book of the Bible: the text is rich enough, layered and convoluted, with a storyline which doubles back on itself, partly told by symbol and cipher, each revealing an aspect of truth. This chapter will confine itself to a bare-bones outline of the plot and the symbols employed, and an understanding of the chronology of events (not fully sequential).

Please attempt the book yourself.

It carries, as I said, a blessing.

Please also note, the Revelation is *of* Jesus Christ *to* John.

The Book of Revelation opens with John, a prisoner on the isle of Patmos, a little island off Asia Minor (modern Turkey). He is occupied with letters of encouragement to the early church when a great voice behind him says, *I am Alpha and Omega, the first and the last*, (ch.1:11).

John turns. He sees seven golden candlesticks and a figure walking amidst them whose face is as the sun, with eyes like flame and feet like burning brass and whose voice is as the sound of many waters. John faints, and is lifted up by this figure who says, *Fear not; I am the first and the last: I am he that liveth and was dead; and, behold, I am alive for evermore, Amen; and have the keys of hell and of death,* (ch.1:17-18).

It is Jesus.

Jesus commands John to write down his messages to the seven churches, represented by the seven golden candlesticks. These letters would more accurately be described as a report card on performance: points for praise, areas for improvement, sometimes a stern caution. The seven churches, in the order in which they appear, are as under:

- Ephesus: has forsaken its first love
- Smyrna: will be persecuted
- Pergamos: needs to repent
- Thyatira: has accepted false teaching
- Sardis: has fallen asleep
- Philadelphia: has endured patiently
- Laodicea: has lukewarm faith

It is sometimes taught that the churches are 'church ages' i.e. periods that the church has passed through, arriving finally at Laodicea, the lukewarm church of today. This ignores the essential premise of Revelation as an end time disclosure, not history. It is also historically inaccurate to state that the first church, Ephesus, had strayed from their first love (Jesus); in fact the early church suffered persecution and hardship because of their unshakeable faith in Jesus. A more valid understanding of the text is to see the churches of Revelation as the types of people who will populate the last days.

In short, you are the 'church.'

Not your husband or wife, not your children, not your family or friends, not your neighbours, not your co-workers, not the church that you (perhaps) attend.

Just you, yourself.

To those who have endured and withstood the pressures of the world and kept his word, Jesus speaks words of praise (Philadelphia, ch.3:7); to those who suffer persecution he offers the crown of life (Smyrna, ch.2:8; they are among the Elect, they shall not suffer a second death); to those who have strayed into false doctrine and false belief Jesus speaks a stern warning (Thyatira, ch.2:18; Ahab, seventh king of Israel, was introduced by his wife Jezebel to the worship of idols); a wake-up call is issued to those who have fallen asleep while waiting for him (Sardis, ch.3:1; it recalls the story of the ten virgins, an end-times parable); he warns against the Nicolaitans, a sect who wandered back to pagan gods while trying to hold on to Jesus, worshipping both (Ephesus, ch.2:1); he reprimands those who are of lukewarm faith, observing the gestures but without true belief or commitment (Laodicea, ch.3:14).

To one 'church,' Jesus utters a strong command to repent (Pergamos, ch.2:12; identified by Christ as 'the seat of Satan'). The ruins of this ancient city lie in the Izmir province of Turkey. It was here that the German engineer and archaeologist, Carl Humann, discovered the altar frieze of the throne of Zeus (also called the Pergamon Altar), in 1878. It was subsequently shipped, stone by stone, to Berlin, Germany, where it currently exists as a museum. Hitler had the platforms for his great rallies modelled on the Pergamon Altar. Jesus's strongest rebuke is to this church.

The letters to the churches are a final warning and appeal, in the last days.

The letters cover chapters 1-3 of Revelation; chapters 4-11 present end times as seen from heaven. John is carried up in the spirit before the throne of Almighty God. He describes the blazing splendour of God and the four living creatures about His throne (ch.4:6-7), identical to the symbols on the four lead banners about the tabernacle of God in the wilderness (Num. 2:2-54); and Ezekiel's vision of the four living creatures (Eze.1:10). The Almighty One holds a book in His hand, secured by seven seals; but none of the host who stand before him is found worthy to break open the seals till the slain Lamb appears. He takes the book from the hand of God, and all the host of heaven and the living creatures bow down in worship.

One by one, Jesus breaks the seals.

The first four seals are the four horses of the Apocalypse:

- the white horse, false christs; false teaching within the body of Christ; false prophets claiming revelation from God; the advancement of alternative worship systems; in the final run-up white as a symbol of false peace, *For when they shall say, Peace and safety, then sudden destruction cometh upon them,* (1Thess.5:3)

- the red horse, war; this horse has been running a long time but the destructive power of nuclear technology dwarfs previous carnage; red symbolising blood/violence; the colour also linked to communism, a (relatively) new political philosophy enforced through wide-scale genocide

- the black horse, poverty and pestilence; symbolically 'in the black' signifying money; the U.S. dollar, base currency of international trade, was completely delinked from the gold standard in 1971, with the consequent evils of fiscal manipulation, inflation, stagflation; globalisation (a relatively new concept) carrying the economic disaster of one country to the next; *a measure of wheat for a penny,* ch.6:6, a denarius/penny representing a day's wage for the common man (Matt.20:2), i.e. a hand to mouth existence; *see thou hurt not the oil and the wine,* ch.6:6; wine suggesting luxury, economic disparity; (does 'black' oil precipitate the final war?); the colour also linked to fascist ideology; pestilence represented by the onslaught of new illnesses like AIDS, Ebola, Zika; radiation fallout

- the green horse (mistranslated as 'pale,' the original Greek is *kloros*, green); linked to death and hell, with power over a fourth of the earth

The fifth seal shows John the souls of the martyrs crying out for vengeance; they are asked to wait, others are expected (the future of these souls is clarified in ch.20:4, *and they lived and reigned with Christ a thousand years*). The persecution of the Church and the rapidly pounding hooves of the four horses come together in the great tribulation, a three-and-a-half-year period assigned to the antichrist.

The breaking of the first five seals may be seen as incremental and progressive.

The sixth seal, however, is singular and definitive,

And lo, there was a great earthquake; and the sun became black as sackcloth of hair, and the moon became as blood; And the stars of heaven fell unto the earth...And the heaven departed as a scroll when it is rolled together; and every mountain and island were moved out of their places, (ch.6:12-14).

Isaiah's prophecy echoes the sixth seal, *Therefore I will shake the heavens and the earth shall move out of her place, in the wrath of the LORD of hosts, and in the day of his fierce anger,* (Isaiah 13: 13).

Scientists agree that what is described here is a pole shift.

Slow and minor movement of the magnetic north has been known and recorded for many years, attributed to the earth's molten core; but a magnetic pole shift which is abrupt and fairly rapid would result in natural disasters, possibly EMP (electro-magnetic pulse) outage, collapsing electronic equipment and communication, enough for chaos.

Complete magnetic reversal multiplies danger.

A crustal pole shift would be catastrophic.

Let me briefly digress from the Bible to our modern world.

In the 1960s, Chilean astronomer Carlos Muñoz Ferrada identified a hybrid comet-planet (with the requisite mass of a planet, plus a tail, hence hybrid), travelling towards earth on an immense elliptical orbit. He named this object, Hercolubus; it has since been called Nibiru or Planet X; (please google Ferrada's last interview, it is instructive).

Ferrada hypothesized a binary sun system, a theory which is still considered viable today (accounting for the faint wobble in earth's axis). He judged that this 'hybrid' would pass about 8.7 million miles from earth but cutting through the same plane as earth, and visible on its near approach with the naked eye. Depending on the time of its crossing, earth could experience the gravitational pull of this object estimated at 7-10 times the size of earth; alternately, the earth could run into its debris field; if so, earth's gravity would pull passing debris towards itself. Ferrada's work received peer validation. It was reported in science journals and covered by the popular press until the early 1970s when the subject abruptly went dark.

Planet X, on its approach path, could account for environmental change and volcanic disturbance, both on the increase. The last decade has seen a steady re-awakening of volcanoes in the Ring of Fire, including ash plumes and lava flows in Mt Sinabung (Indonesia), Mt Ontake (Japan), Villarrica and Calbuco (Chile), Mt Etna (Sicily); simmering activity in Santa Maria (Gautemala), molten carbon in the geothermal maze beneath Yellowstone Park (U.S.A.) and magma shifts in the long dormant super-volcano, Campi Flegrei (Italy).

Planet X, on its approach, would affect magnetic

fields and trigger seismic activity. There has been a strong upward tick in the frequency and magnitude of seismic quakes as witnessed by quake inspired tsunamis in the Indian Ocean (2004) and off N-E Japan (2011, the Fukushima disaster); the immense slip-quake off Sumatra (2012), which split a tectonic plate; and the high magnitude earthquakes of Bhuj (India), Bam (Iran), Java (Indonesia), Port-au-prince (Haiti), and Sichuan (China), plus dozens of significant lower magnitude quakes.

Among the markers of his return, Christ lists –

Famines, and pestilences, and earthquakes in diverse places. All these are the beginning of sorrows, (Matt. 24:7-8).

[N.B. The beginning of sorrows, a euphemism for childbirth; it correlates the increasing strength and rapidity of contractions to the pointers listed.]

Planet X could also explain the seed banks and unprecedented number of underground bunkers, almost cities, dug by governments around the world in the last quarter century, including 'doomsday condos' in secure parts of the world. Who will they shelter? Revelation identifies them, *And the kings of the earth, and the great men, and the rich men, and the chief captains, and the mighty men, and every bondsman and every free man, hid themselves in the dens and in the rocks of the mountains; And said to the mountains and rocks, Fall on us, and hide us from the face of him that sitteth on the throne, and from the wrath of the Lamb: For the great day of his wrath is come; and who shall be able to stand?* (ch.6:15-17).

A pole flip or geomagnetic reversal, is today theorised as a real possibility by many scientists. Rune Floberghagen, European Space Agency's SWARM manager, stated that the earth's magnetic field is losing strength at an alarming rate, ten times faster than originally projected – able to map the changing fields, scientists are unable to identify a reason for the change nor explain the South Atlantic Anomaly. The reports, in 2014 and 2016, received little media coverage.

On March 14, 2017 *Tech Times* ran an article headed, 'Earth's Magnetic Pole Reversal: What Are The Consequences?', indicating patches deep within the earth's crust already showing reversal.

Maybe global warming is something beyond man.

Not that we do not play a part.

Solar panels, (promoted as man's best alternative to oil, coal and gas in the fight against carbon emission and environmental pollution) use nitrogen trifluoride in the manufacture of photovoltaic cells. NF3s are a toxic greenhouse gas. NF3 emissions have increased 1057% over the last twenty-five years compared with a 5% increase in carbon dioxide. Worse, NF3s are 17,200 times more potent than carbon dioxide. The news was part of a U.S. federal data release, (statistics quoted by the *Daily Caller*, March 3, 2017).

The black humour of NF3s is a bit like nuclear energy. Nuclear energy was strongly pushed in the 1950s and 60s but the waste was never planned for – other than burying it deep in the earth for future generations to handle. But the future is now. The Fukushima Daiichi disaster, March 2011, released radioactive waste (including the water-soluble isotope Cesium-137) into the Pacific Ocean; the toxic plume has been slowly drifting these last six years towards the Canadian and U.S. western seaboard.

To return to John's vision of the sixth seal –

Following the breaking of the sixth seal, John hears an order given: the earth and sea are not to be hurt till those who serve God are sealed in their foreheads; 1,44,000 in all, twelve thousand men from each of the twelve tribes of Jacob. The list excludes the tribe of Dan, but maintains a total of twelve by allotting a double portion to Joseph's descendants.

These 'sealed' men are taught a song no one else can sing, the everlasting gospel of God. They are sent to earth to preach his Holy Word amid the plagues of the Trumpet Judgements, but they are protected from the plagues by the seal of God. A precursor of this event is the final pre-Exodus plague; the seal of protection matches the blood of the slain lamb on the doorposts of the Hebrew homes, passed over (untouched) by the angel of death.

[N.B. The exclusion of Dan has led to the belief

that the antichrist will be a descendant of this tribe; this notion is fostered by the symbol on Dan's banner, an eagle with a snake in its beak. Interestingly, Mount Hermon – straddling the Syria-Lebanon border, its southern slope running down to the Golan Heights – lies in the territory assigned to the lost tribe of Dan. Apocryphal texts name Mount Hermon as the place where the pre-Flood fallen angels set foot on earth, *the angels which kept not their first estate, but left their own habitation* (Jude 1:6, 2 Peter 2:4); it is a short distance from Ba'albek in Lebanon, ancient worship site of Ba'al. This sector of the Golan Heights holds the prehistoric stone monument Gilgal Refaim or Wheel of Giants, a supposed burial ground; it lies in ancient Bashan ruled by Og, *of the remnant of the giants,* (Deut.3:11, 2:20-21; also Gen.6:4, Num.13:32; 1Sam.17:4; 2Sam.21:20; 1Chr.11:23). Taken in context, these scattered accounts overlay each other and knit together, suggesting forbidden interaction and pockets of altered DNA. These accounts also explain difficult parts of the Old Testament, especially in Deuteronomy, Samuel and Chronicles, where the Israelites were commanded to wipe out certain tribes, taking nothing as plunder (no living thing, no grain), while others were shown mercy.]

Following the sealing of the 1,44,000 John sees a multitude in heaven, *a great multitude, which no man could number, of all nations, and kindreds, and people, and tongues,* (ch.7:9). John is informed that they have come through the great tribulation and been martyred for Christ; the event recalls St. Paul, *the dead in Christ shall rise first,* (1Thess.4:16).

And with this vision of the multitude, the seventh seal is opened.

Seven angels with seven trumpets appear.

The first trumpet sounds.

If the sixth seal marks a pole shift, then the time between the sixth and seven seal will be very short because the first four trumpet judgements are a natural consequence of a pole shift. A pole flip or even a sudden slippage would cause chaos and deaths too many to count. In this confusion, will the Elect be gathered to God, caught up with a trumpet blast?

It seems likely.

Who are the Elect? Those righteous in God's sight.

In God's sight, not the world's –

Then shall the righteous answer him saying, Lord, when saw we thee an hungered and fed thee? or thirsty and gave thee drink? (Matt.25:37).

Confusion and calamity are plot elements of the sixth seal: the missing, the dead, disrupted communication and general chaos permit unbelievers to continue in unbelief, not realising the (spiritual) event which has taken place, considering themselves 'lucky' to be alive rather than the reverse. The prophet Isaiah writes, *The righteous perish... none considering that the righteous is taken away from the evil to come,* (Isaiah 57:1).

Those who are left continue unaware.

Unawareness, and the consequences of unawareness, form a persistent theme in Revelation; a judgement on those who do not/will not watch –

And in them is fulfilled the prophecy of Esaias, which saith, By hearing ye shall hear and shall not understand; and seeing ye shall see and shall not perceive, (Matt.13:14-15; Mark 4:12; Acts 28:26; Isaiah 6:9-10).

The Feasts of Our Lord, presented earlier in this book, suggest a period of time between Trumpets and Atonement, permitting repentance and a return to God (this fits well with the arrival of the sealed men of God who will preach the everlasting gospel; their words break the spiritual atrophy of those who can still hear, awakening them to truth and repentance and marking a huge revival in faith); how *much* time between Trumpets and Atonement, we do not know. God alone will decide when the doors of heaven finally shut.

Is there any difference between the Elect and those who follow later? The Elect live again and reign with Christ a thousand years, (ch.20:6).

The repentant who are saved will sleep in death for a thousand years till the Books of Life are opened and the White Throne Judgement, (ch.20:12). A second death is mentioned which has no power over the Elect (ch.20:6; also the letter to Smyrna, ch.2:11); also mentioned is a brief release of Satan at the end of a thousand years to tempt the nations a final time against God, (ch.20:7-10); it is not clear if the repentant who sleep in death are also released to be re-tried and test their repentance – is this the second death that is mentioned?

But the ungodly shall continue in idolatrous worship and blasphemy of God, and in the practice of sorcery, fornication, murder and theft (ch.9:21), until the final day decreed by God. The element of surprise continues (for them) till the end.

John's vision moves to the Day of God's wrath.

Old Testament prophets echo Revelation in its description –

Alas for the day! for the day of the LORD is at hand, and as a destruction from the Almighty it shall come, (Joel 1:15).

That day is a day of wrath, a day of trouble and distress, [of] clouds and thick darkness... they shall walk like blind men because they have sinned against the LORD: and their blood shall be poured out as dust, and their flesh as the dung, (Zeph.1:15-17).

Howl ye; for the day of the LORD is at hand... For the stars of heaven and the constellations thereof shall not give their light: the sun shall be darkened in his going forth, and the moon shall not cause her light to shine. And I will punish the world for their evil, (Isaiah 13:6-11).

How long is the Day of Wrath?

In prophetic terms it could equal one year but the devastation of the judgements suggest a shorter timespan; the fifth trumpet indicates a period of five months. The Great Awakening and the period of Atonement appear to mingle with the start of the Trumpet Judgements, as under:

- first trumpet, first vial: hail and fire with blood (of birds?) falls on earth, a third of the trees burned up (a rip in the atmospheric veil? a coronal mass ejection?)
- second trumpet, second vial: a burning mountain (meteor? volcano?) cast into the sea, a third of the sea becomes blood (of fish?)
- third trumpet, third vial: a burning star (asteroid?) falls to earth, a third of the rivers turn bitter; the star is named Wormwood
- fourth trumpet, fourth vial: a third part of the sun is darkened, so too the moon and stars, *the day shone not for a third part of it, and the night likewise* (ch.8:12); does the asteroid hit cause the earth to spin faster, a 24-hour day shortening to 18 hours?
- fifth trumpet, fifth vial, 1st woe: a star falls from heaven, *and to him was given the key of the bottomless pit* (ch.9:1); scorpion-like locusts emerge to torment mankind for five months,

and in those days men shall seek death, and shall not find it (ch.9:6). [N.B. The king of the bottomless pit is Apollyon, Greek god of the sun; his other symbols include the bow (false christ?), lyre, python, raven and swan]
- sixth trumpet, sixth vial, 2nd woe: the call of a two hundred-million-man army to war (ch.9:16; 16:14); a third of mankind is killed (ch.9:18)

The trumpets are briefly halted in John's vision by the descent of a mighty angel who stands upon the land and sea, declaring, *there should be time no longer* (ch.10:6). Meanwhile, on earth, God's two witnesses are killed in Jerusalem amid rejoicing (ch.11:3-11); their bodies lie in the streets for three and a half days before they are suddenly resurrected.

[N.B. Some see the two witnesses as Enoch and Elijah, the only two men in the Bible who do not die but are carried up to God; the two witnesses fulfil the prophecy of Zechariah 4:2-14.]

With the resurrection of the two men the seventh trumpet is blown:

- seventh trumpet, seventh vial, 3rd woe: a mighty earthquake; the cities of the world fall amid hail, *every stone about the weight of a talent* (ch.16:21; a talent, about seventy pounds), with thundering and lightning

And there were great voices in heaven, saying, *The kingdoms of this world are become the kingdoms of our Lord and of his Christ: and he shall reign for ever and ever,* (ch.11:15).

For beginners, the Book of Revelation is disjointed and confusing, not merely because of the symbols used but because of its chronology.

Put simply, chapters 4-11 show end times from heaven; chapters 12-16 replay end times from earth. It is followed by zoom chapters on Mystery Babylon and Armageddon (chapters 17-18); then Wedding Preparations and the Victory of the Lamb (chapter 19); finally the White Throne Judgement and Millennial Kingdom (chapters 20-22). Added in the replay are symbolic descriptions of the antichrist, the false prophet and Mystery Babylon, three entities that rule the last days. The symbols work as identifying markers, enabling those who study the word of God to understand and recognise these players when they will eventually step forth, and so safeguard their souls.

Chapter 12 opens the replay of tribulation as seen from earth: *And there appeared a great wonder in heaven* (ch.12:1), it is the image of a woman travailing in pain and the birth of a male child (already discussed). The birth is followed by a war in heaven. Satan and his cohorts are tossed to earth; Satan is filled with anger knowing his time is short.

And now the visions of John and Daniel meet.

John sees *a beast rise up out of the sea, having seven heads and ten horns, and upon his horns ten crowns, and upon his heads the names of blasphemy. And the beast I saw was unto a leopard, and his feet were as the feet of a bear, and his mouth as the mouth of a lion: and the dragon gave him his power and his seat and great authority,* (ch.13:1-2).

The beast is straight from the second vision of Daniel, a composite of the animals representing the four kingdoms (thus seven heads and ten horns).

The defining elements of those past kingdoms define our modern world: the heady egoism of our me-first 'selfie' culture (self-deification, Babylon); intrusive documentation (administration, Medo-Persia); money delinked from intrinsic value (bronze coinage, Greece); close control tempered by benefits (military might, the concept of 'bread and circuses' first introduced by Rome – *panis et circenses*, Juvenal, Satire X, c.100 A.D., maintaining a quiescent citizenry with free wheat and great spectacle).

The beast is shown as both system and man.

Each component of the beast system (institution), helps empower the beast (man, antichrist) in a symbiotic relationship. The multiple heads of the beast are manifestations of these institutions in the world; they do not exist sequentially but at the same time. So too the beast-man, though foreshadowed in history, is now fully manifest in one individual, the antichrist.

Revelation proceeds from a description of the beast to its actions (ch.13:5-7). These actions are identical to the little horn in Daniel:

- he has a mouth speaking great things and blasphemies
- he makes war with the saints (the people of God)
- he has power to continue forty and two months

A new element now appears, *And I beheld another beast coming up out of the earth; and he had two horns like a lamb, and he spake as a dragon. And he exerciseth all the power of the first beast before him,* (ch.13:11-12).

This new beast is the false prophet; the word 'lamb' suggests he will present himself as a mild and likeable person but his words promote the agenda of Satan. The false prophet validates the antichrist in a dark replay of John the Baptist and Christ. The false prophet works miracles, including giving life to an 'image' (statue/picture, hologram?) of the antichrist; he calls down fire from heaven.

These activities tie into the Olivet discourse of *great signs and wonders; insomuch that, if it were possible, they shall deceive the very elect,* (Matt.24:24).

As already stated, the central purpose of Revelation is to lay out these end-time events in advance so that we may not be deceived.

The antichrist, swollen with power, now seeks to mark all men in their right hand or in their forehead. Prophecy scholars relate this mark to the implant of a technological device – maybe an RFID chip under the skin which will hardwire the recipient to the World Wide Web; a virtual immersion headset which alters perceived reality beyond its actual use; or an invasive 'health monitor' apparatus; but varied other possibilities exist including DNA alteration. Taking this mark is equated with the loss of one's soul (ch.20:4); but those who refuse the mark face hardship, for *no man might buy or sell, save he that had the mark, or the name of the beast, or the number of his name. Here is wisdom. Let him that has understanding count the number of the beast; for it is the number of a man; and his number is Six hundred threescore and six,* (ch.13:17-18).

And here we arrive at 666, the number of corrupted man under the control of Satan.

666 is the upside down and reversed reflection of 999, (9 representing finality, judgement and the perfect movement of God; a number tripled is the quality of that number reinforced). Upside down and reversed is important. The mirror image of certain numbers that we met in the first chapter of this book is a side to side reflection; full upside down imagery/numbers is linked to the dark arts of scrying and divination; upside down and reversed is linked to satanic practice.

The word 'mark' in the Greek text is 'charagma', (*Strong's Concordance* no. G5480), meaning a stamp, sign, etching, engraving; the subtext draws a connection to a coin impress or branding iron providing undeniable identification and/or irrefutable connection between parties.

Multiple interpretations have been assigned to the number 666, too numerous and contentious to mention here. Instead of divisive speculation, know that the antichrist will reveal himself through his actions when he finally steps into his role. An identifying factor will be the introduction of a controlled worship system. Worship is central to the antichrist; a coerced worship so that *as many as would not worship the image of the beast should be killed,* (ch.13:15). Aiding implementation of a one world religion is current globalist philosophy (though damaged by Brexit and the Trump victory), which seeks a one world order. Globalism, initially presented as a populist move, has actually concentrated the world's wealth and power in the hands of a few, a tiny fraction of a half percentile. At the World Economic Forum in Davos, Switzerland, January 2017, the U.K. *Guardian* reported the warning of Chinese Premier Xi Jinping against 'populism' (the supposed foundation of communist theory), his remarks strongly supported by all member nations present. Globalism offers an easy path to a one world currency, also on the horizon. Growing economic disparity, restive BRIC economies and a pumped-up U.S. dollar are all factors of chaos that could push the world toward the beast.

Let us return to John's vision of end times.

The crushing power of the antichrist and false prophet, detailed in chapter 13, is now cut by a great awakening among the people of God, chapter 14. John sees a Lamb on mount Sion; with him are the 1,44,000 sealed men of God (already discussed; chapter 14 draws a link with chapter 7). It suggests that Jesus will accompany his men into (spiritual) battle – but he is still a lamb, sealed off from our recognition; he is not yet the lion of Judah. Remember the earlier caution: Jesus will only show himself in glory on the last day; do not be deceived by any other, (see the Olivet discourse, Matt.24:26).

John's vision now moves to three mighty angelic announcements (ch.14:7-10):

- fear God, for his hour of his judgement is come
- Babylon is fallen
- whoever bears the mark of the beast shall taste the wrath of God

This opens the final judgement.

The vine of the earth (not the true vine) is cast into the winepress of God's wrath and the seven vials of God's wrath are poured out upon the desolate to complete the decreed desolation, spoken of in Daniel.

As the vials are emptied, the earth is scorched, the seas and rivers turn to blood, men break out with festering sores; darkness falls upon the seat of the beast and the river Euphrates runs dry. Three unclean spirits emerge from the dragon, the antichrist and the false prophet calling the nations to war.

It is the battle of Armageddon.

The earth shall quake before them; the heavens shall tremble: the sun and moon shall be dark, and the stars shall withdraw their shining, And the LORD shall utter his voice before his army: for his camp is very great: for he is strong that execueth his word: for the day of the LORD is great and very terrible; and who can abide it? (Joel 2:10-11).

The seventh vial is emptied and a voice from heaven cries, It is done (ch.16:17). Once again, John describes thunders and lightning, hail and a mighty earthquake, so great, *that every island fled away and the mountains were not found,* (ch.16:20).

And so we come to the 'zoom' chapters on Mystery Babylon and Armageddon. Who is Mystery Babylon? She is described as a beautiful harlot, richly arrayed in purple and scarlet, decked with precious stones. She holds a golden cup of abominations in her hand, (abomination and harlotry are pseudonyms for false worship). She is drunk with the blood of the saints and martyrs of Jesus Christ, (ch.17:6). Her role is the seduction of nations into worship of the beast. She is also described as the mother of harlots (ch.17:5, i.e. other systems of false worship have grown from her false worship), and she carries the title of her harlotry and mystery on her forehead; as queen, she *sitteth on many waters,* (ch.17:1, explained as people, multitudes and tongues, ch.17:15), and *reigneth over the kings of the earth,* (ch.17:18).

And she rides the beast.

Who is she?

One element of identification lies in the colour of her garments. Interestingly, these colours exactly accord with the commanded colours around the tabernacle of God in the wilderness, the curtain hangings, the veil, as also the robes of the high priest (Exo.26:1; 27:16; 28:5) – with one exception, there is no blue (see Chris White, *Mystery Babylon Study*).

Blue is the colour of purity and right standing with God: Ezekiel references the throne of God as a sapphire, (Eze.1:26); Numbers tells us that the Israelites were commanded to put a *ribband of blue* in the fringe of their garments to recall the commandments of God, (Num.15:38).

John is struck by the splendour of the woman.

The angel asks John, *Wherefore didst thou marvel? I will tell thee the mystery of the woman, and of the beast that carrieth her, which hath seven heads and ten horns...*

The seven heads are seven mountains on which the woman sitteth, (ch.17:7-9).

This reference places Babylon as a city on seven mountains. It has drawn immediate attention to Rome and the Vatican, well recognised as the City of Seven Hills – but it is worth noting that Judaism, Islam and Hinduism also have central cities of worship which can claim the distinction of seven hills. Thus:

- Rome: Aventine, Caelian, Capitoline, Esquiline, Palatine, Quirinal, Viminal
- Jerusalem: Gared, Akra, Zion, Goath, Bezetha, Moriah, Ophel
- Mecca: Jabal Safa, Marwa, Siba, Milah, Ma'aya, Hulaya, Ghuzlan
- Tirumal: Seshadri, Neeladri, Garudari, Anjanadri, Vrushabhadri, Narayanadri, Venkatadri

Biblically, the 'great city' is a term most often used for Jerusalem. Jerusalem is the city of God, great before all others, referred to as such in Jeremiah 22:8 and in terms of exaltation throughout the Old Testament, (D. Ragan Ewing, *The Identification of Babylon the Harlot*).

Even accepting this view, ideologically distinct conclusions are drawn.

The preterist view sees Revelation as played out in the past, with Jerusalem and its priestly leadership as the historical harlot, judged and destroyed in 70 A.D. The preterist view is not widely held as Revelation categorically states itself as an end-time unfolding.

The more accepted view places Revelation in the future; but here, too, are divisions. Some see an eschatological identification of the great city following the death of the two witnesses, *And their dead bodies shall lie in the street of the great city, which spiritually is called Sodom and Egypt, where also our Lord was crucified,* (ch.11:8); the splitting of the 'great city' (ch.16:19) is linked to Zechariah 14:4, the splitting of the Mount of Olives. This view is supported by a section of Bible scholarship and in fact goes back to the teaching of the early church and founding fathers like St. Hippolytus of Rome, (170-235 A.D.); it is, however, strongly opposed by many modern scholars who see Jerusalem validated by the New Jerusalem of the millennial kingdom.

Revelation's harlot, however, is not bound to an exclusively religious interpretation. Secular options also exist. Foremost among them is New York: Staten Island, geographically part of the New York area, is situated on seven hills (Fort, Ward, Fox, Grymes, Emerson, Todt and Richmond), with the U.N. easily fulfilling the role of a powerful multi-headed beast with its political, military, educational, financial, health, etc 'heads.' In this interpretation, the League of Nations is seen as the 'wounded' head, whose *deadly wound was healed,* (ch.13:3).

Also popular on the secular list is the E.U.; ironically, Brussels also sits on seven hills (St.

Michielsberg, Koudenberg, Warmoesberg, Kruidtuin, Kuntsberg, Zavel and St.Pietersberg). Supporters of the E.U. as beast point to the old myth and current representation of Europa on a bull (a woman rides the beast), directly outside E.U. headquarters in Brussels, as well as on Euro coinage, declaring it an in-your-face acknowledgement.

Weaker contenders are Athens, Istanbul and Moscow, also on seven hills.

Once researched, the seven hills description, while distinctive, is not as distinctive as it may seem.

After delivering this geographic marker, the angel layers the prophecy to identify the seven mountains as also seven 'kings,' *five are fallen, and one is and the other is not yet come; and when he cometh he must continue a short space, And the beast that was and is not, even he is the eighth and is of the seven, and goeth into perdition,* (ch.17:10-11); this description is immediately layered with another, *and the ten horns which thou sawest are ten kings,* (ch.17:12).

Who are these many kings with diverse numbers?

It is generally agreed that the first use of 'king' signifies 'kingdom' or empire (as in the Book of Daniel, where 'king' and 'kingdom' are used interchangeably). At the time of John's vision five empires had come and gone (Egypt, Assyria, Babylon, Medo-Persia, Greece), one presently existed (Rome); the seventh lay in the future (with the antichrist). The antichrist's kingdom is of 'a short space', forty-two months. The verse, *And the beast that was and is not, even he is the eighth and is of the seven, and goeth into perdition* (ch.17:11), refers to the deadly head wound from which the antichrist recovers in a type of resurrection (once again a dark replay of Christ's resurrection), thus making him both the seventh and eighth.

Some prophecy scholars reject the 'kingdom' interpretation and see the seven kings as actual kings, six manifestations of the antichrist in the past, now fully manifest in the final antichrist. This analysis also has a following.

In the multilayered context of Revelation, both analyses can co-exist.

There is no dispute on the 'horns' of the beast, also called 'kings': they are ten world leaders who have *no kingdom,* (ch.17:12) i.e. their positions are not political, suggesting heads of multinational conglomerates or global institutions; they *have one mind,* (ch.17:13) i.e. are unanimous; they *give their power and strength unto the beast,* (ch.17:13) i.e. the organisations they control are given over to the antichrist for his use. In return these men *receive power as kings one hour with the beast,* (ch.17:12). This passage directly reaffirms the beast as both system and man.

Mystery Babylon, though she rides the beast, does not control the beast. She believes she *sits as a queen… and shall see no sorrow* (ch.18:7); but the horns of the beast hate her and turn on her, *and shall eat her flesh and burn her with fire,* (ch.17:16). Her final judgement is from God, *For her sins have reached unto heaven, and God hath remembered her iniquities… in the cup which she hath filled, fill to her double,* (ch.18:5-6).

Her fall is mighty and swift, *in one hour* (ch.18:19). Traders, their boats still anchored at sea, watch her burn in shocked awe. The 'boats at sea' suggest geographic details for Mystery Babylon – but Rome, Mecca and Jerusalem, as also New York and Brussels, may all be seen from waterways; a narrower clue are the mourners who *cast dust on their heads* (ch.18:19), a sign of grief tied to eastern culture.

Closely following the destruction of this great city is the battle of Armageddon.

As Mystery Babylon is symbolic of false worship, so Armageddon is symbolic of an apocalyptic battle between good and evil, with good finally triumphant. *Three unclean spirits like frogs* (ch.16:13), issue from the mouth of the dragon, the antichrist and the false prophet (this verse explicitly shows Satan as a separate entity from the antichrist, though he empowers the antichrist). These *spirits of devils, working miracles… go forth unto the kings of the earth,* (ch.16:14); it is important to note that the 'wonders' Jesus warned about continue to the very end.

Will the battle of Armageddon actually occur at the place from which this name comes? Har Megiddo, or hill of Megiddo, exists in Northern Israel; a tel, rather than a hill, formed by the ruins of a city being built over repeatedly (excavations have unearthed twenty-six layers of ruins at Megiddo). The ancient city is located near the river Kidron, strategically sited at a pass overlooking the Valley of Jezreel, about sixty miles north of Jerusalem. Some scholars see it as an alternate placement for the palace of the antichrist (Dan.11:45, alternate to Mount Moriah) because it lies between two seas (the Mediterranean Sea and the Sea of Galilee, area of Christ's ministry) and is part of the broken chain of mountains to which Mount Moriah belongs, a splintered off-shoot towards Mt. Carmel, while the main chain carries on to Mt. Lebanon.

Har Megiddo is currently a quiet World Heritage site (figure xv).

The armies of the world gather at Armageddon, two hundred million strong.

In reply to this assembly comes *the noise of a multitude in the mountains… the LORD of hosts mustereth the host of the battle. They come from a far country, from the end of heaven, even the LORD, and the weapons of his indignation,* (Isaiah 13:4-5).

Revelation describes a powerful, conquering figure whose vesture is dipped in blood; across his thigh runs a name, KING OF KINGS AND LORD OF LORDS; out of his mouth issues a fiery sword of vengeance as he treads the winepress of God's wrath.

The carnage is great: blood runs high as a horse's bridle (ch.14:20); birds gather to feast upon the flesh of kings (ch.19:18).

The image of birds feasting on carrion is also found in Jesus's description of end time –

Wheresoever the body is, thither will the eagles be gathered together, (Luke 17:34; Matt.24:28).

Do 'eagles' hint at the participants of this great battle? The eagle was a pre-eminent symbol of ancient

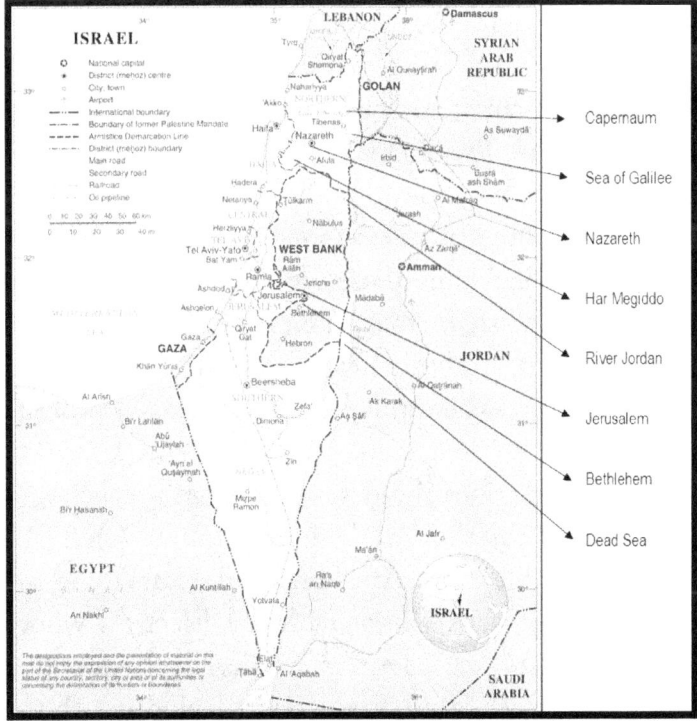

Fig. xv: Map of Israel with areas of biblical significance indicated

Rome; today it appears on the seal/coat of arms of many nations, principally Albania, Armenia, Austria, Egypt, Germany, Iraq, Libya, Mexico, Moldova, Montenegro, Palestine, Poland, Romania, Russia, Serbia, South Sudan, Syria, Thailand, U.A.E., Ukraine, U.S.A., Uzbekistan, Yemen. The eagle is used in the Bible to show swiftness (Jer.4:13; Deut.28:49), but also as a bird of judgement that will devour, *He shall come as an eagle against the house of the LORD, because they have transgressed my covenant,* (Hosea 8:1); *they shall fly as the eagle that hasteth to eat,* (Habakkuk 1:8).

Armageddon ends with Christ's victory.

The antichrist and false prophet are consigned to the lake of fire. The dragon is bound in chains and cast into the bottomless pit for a thousand years; after this time he is loosed 'a little season,' ch.20:3 (presumably to try for a final time those whose last minute cry to God has saved them, but whose repentance is born of fear, not faith); after this 'little season' he too is cast into the lake of fire where the antichrist and false prophet still burn.

John describes the descent of a new heaven and a new earth for the first had passed away (ch.21:1); he describes the joyous Wedding of the Lamb and the millennial reign of Christ with the Elect on whom *the second death hath no power, but shall be priests of God and of Christ,* (ch.20:6). Revelation concludes with the opening of the Book of Life and the White Throne judgement (ch.20:12).

The end, for the people of God, is rejoicing and reward.

The end is rejoicing – but before we can get there we have to live here. The deception will be great, the plot and the players not as easily recognisable as in the book.

The last days are a time of testing.

A time when men *will put darkness for light, and light for darkness,* (Isaiah 5:20).

Even as late as chapter 16, when the armies of the world are being gathered to Armageddon, John records this warning from Christ –

Behold, I come as a thief. Blessed is he that watcheth, (Rev.16:15).

It is a warning which Christ issued while he still walked the earth –

Watch ye therefore… lest coming suddenly [the master] find you sleeping. And what I say unto you I say unto all, Watch, (Mark 13:35-37).

7 – the Challenge of Free Will and an Age of Deceit

This know also, that in the last days perilous times shall come. For men shall be lovers of their own selves... boasters... blasphemers... unthankful, unholy, Without natural affection, truce breakers, false accusers, incontinent, fierce, despisers of those that are good... lovers of pleasures more than lovers of God; Having a form of godliness, but denying the power thereof... Ever learning, and never able to come to a knowledge of the truth, (2 Timothy 3:1-7).

Notwithstanding the noisy clamour of this world, there are some among us who can still hear the muffled drumbeat of fulfilled prophecy and they wonder, are we living in the last days?

Others ask, will those days ever happen?

And yet others ask, can we even know if we are living in the last days until the last day really comes?

Good questions, all.

Let us take them to scripture because the answer

lies there: the Bible not only describes the last day but the last one thousand two hundred and sixty days, Revelation's end-time plot. Scattered through the Old and New Testament is a preview of the conditions leading up to that time, a convergence of individual strands that knit together. When those conditions come to pass, when a pattern emerges from the confused ball of yarn with its multicoloured strands, then we may recognise the time and know that we are close, even at the doors.

This chapter will look at those conditions.

It will place prophecy vis-à-vis our world today with the primary focus on science and technology viewed from an eschatological perspective. The information provided is open to personal exploration; it offers points for research; if you are not familiar with any of the terms or ideas expressed in this chapter please go the indicated source and/or a credited site for validation.

But before we move to the broad picture let us first consider a narrow one – our part in an end-time plot that is tied to an all-pervasive atmosphere of deceit.

Do we really have a role to play?

Do we truly have choice?

The question takes us back to the Feasts of Our Lord and the swinging pendulum of choice and freewill – a thorny thicket, but let us venture in.

The Bible is filled with stories of choice – from

Adam and Eve in Eden, to Abraham's sacrifice, to the Israelites dancing around the golden calf, every story in the Bible reflects a choice. So too, in life, we are faced with constant choice: which school? which career? which partner? Some choices are life altering and some are not; some choices are good, others less so. On our list of choice is the salvation offered by Jesus Christ, a free gift which we may accept or reject, a choice we make by exercising our free will.

Deep philosophies have been expounded on these dual concepts of choice and freewill. Indeed, on this side, we see darkly, as through smoke; shadows of a reality, glimpsed and gone.

But sometimes a story can nutshell a truth.

I want to put before you an imagined scenario.

Imagine a distant kingdom far, far away; and a supreme ruler, all powerful and all just.

Imagine a man raised by the supreme ruler to a position of power. He has been given much but wants more; he stirs up rebellion.

The rebellion is put down.

The rebel is brought before the supreme ruler, his governing council and the great assembly.

The rebel accuses the supreme ruler of unfairness; he declares that, in a fair fight, he would have won; but because the supreme ruler is all powerful, he (the rebel) lost.

The supreme ruler, being just, discusses the accusation with his council members. He answers the accusation by suggesting an even playing field through free will: in a limited setting, for a limited time, he will permit complete freedom of choice without intervention; but there is a cost to the experiment, the price will be eternity.

The rebel grabs the offer. He is an arrogant man with a mouth that speaks great things. His pride disregards the cost to himself; he does not consider the cost to others. He begins making demands: he (the rebel) must be present on the playing field, but not the supreme ruler; if the supreme ruler is present, he (the rebel) will be overshadowed; it is unfair to him (the rebel). The council agrees that the rebel cannot match the supreme ruler; but the supreme ruler cannot be absent, some alterative must be found. The supreme ruler decides to write a set of rules in stone and a book to guide the participants.

The son of the supreme ruler offers to go down at halftime to offer sustenance.

The supreme ruler accepts his son's offer. He asks the great assembly, are there volunteers?

Men and women step forward: the best, as in an Amazing Race or the Olympics.

The rebel is afraid of the line-up. He craftily plays to their personal pride. It is too easy, he declares – unless their memories are wiped clean.

The volunteers, confident of their ability, agree.

But the supreme ruler demurs: the volunteers are at risk; he will send men from time to time to remind the players of the consequence of this tournament; he will send an invisible spirit to strengthen those who seek help; the accuser must equally disclose the consequence of choice to those he seeks to turn.

The rebel tries to avoid the rule of disclosure.

The council insists.

The rebel finally selects entertainment to reveal intention; but, to balance the presence of the invisible spirit, he bargains for temporal power and a subtle tongue. The supreme ruler splits the rebel's tongue so that the volunteers may be visually alerted to the accuser's presence; and the gifts and bribes the accuser uses to gain adherents will carry a set of symbols, fixed symbols that do not change over time, by which he may be recognised.

The rules are deemed fair by the council members.

And so events are put in motion.

Imagination, yes. I said so upfront. And a thorny thicket, that too –

Let us consider it, however.

When handed a case, the investigator seeks a hypothesis which accounts for all known factors in the case; once he meets this goal, it is called a working hypothesis. The hypothesis put forward here is not new. It has been used in both classical and popular literature. Almost five hundred years ago a playwright wrote, *All this world's a stage, and all the men and women merely players…* [Shakespeare, *As You Like It*, Act II, Scene vii].

The far-away kingdom is an imagined scenario;

As You Like It is fiction, true enough; and the film, *The Matrix*, is just that, a film.

But truth reaches us in many forms.

Gabriel's prologue to the end-time prophecy in Daniel is a battle between spiritual powers.

The Apostle Paul defined this same battle in Ephesians, *For we wrestle not against flesh and blood, but against principalities, against powers, against rulers of the darkness of this world, against spiritual wickedness in high places. Wherefore take unto you the whole armour of God, that ye may be able to withstand in the evil day, and having done all, to stand* (Eph.6:12-13).

You are a participant in an epic battle.

Will you re-study the rules? Will you review your strategy? Will you recognise the symbols of deceit and return in victory? … or will you be deluded by a wolf in sheep's clothing, by falsehood garbed as truth, by evil cloaked as good?

In Thessalonians Paul writes, *Prove all things; hold fast that which is good* (1Thess.5:20).

Validate what you read and hear, so that you may make an informed choice. Because you will have to stand by the choice you make.

This is the challenge and consequence of freewill.

The nonstop news cycle of the twenty-first century is filled with oppressive reports of turmoil and violence, hostile nationalism, economic malpractice, the destabilisation of the family unit and the destruction of social mores; there are accounts of strange illnesses; images of wildfires, floods and drought; sinkholes and tsunamis; natural disasters and manmade tragedies.

Sitting on the Mount of Olives, Jesus speaks of a world which will precede his Second Coming, one we can recognise in part: wars, famines, earthquakes, these are 'the beginning of sorrows.' The disciples listen anxiously. They fear the departure of their leader, they are eager for his return; they ask – *what shall be the sign of thy coming, and of the end of the world? And Jesus answered and said unto them, Take heed that no man deceive you,* (Matt. 24:3-4).

There will be wars, yes.

Earthquakes and famines, that too.

But the single greatest defining feature of the end zone is deception.

What sort of deception?

Let us start with the most basic tool of deception, the lie.

Are you aware of the 'big lie' technique devised in the run up to World War II and laid out by Adolf Hitler in his autobiography? It promotes, as a propaganda tool, a distortion of truth, so immense, that the unbelievable is accepted; then 'even though the facts which prove this [lie] to be so may be brought clearly to their [the public's] mind, they will still doubt…' [Hitler, *Mein*

Kampf, 1925, vol 1, ch. x].

Make it big, tell it often. This is the paradigm laid out for the last days.

The lie is the first resort of –

Truce breakers, false accusers... (2Tim.3:3).

[They] call evil good and good evil, (Isaiah 5:20).

For when they shall say peace and safety, then sudden destruction cometh, (1Thes. 5:2-3).

August 2016 saw the launch of the world's first quantum satellite by China, with quantum key encryption. The launch presages an umbrella network for Asia-Europe in the near future. Xinhua, China's state news agency, stated that the device could also be used 'to teleport data into space... and conduct experiments on the bizarre features of quantum theories, such as entanglement,' [*Quartz*, Aug.16, 2016]. Q-k encryption was conceived as a tool against cyber hacking; but, in offshoot, it could enforce an instantaneous lockdown of free communication.

In October 2016, ICANN – which handles internet domain names – was freed from U.S. Department of Commerce oversight.

The year 2016 also witnessed a huge clash between mainstream media and alternative media with allegations of 'fake news' by both sides. It exposed increasing censorship of widely used social media sites amid claims of distorted SERPs (Search Engine Results Pages), blocked accounts and trending algorithms compromised by human agency. Disinformation and/or the dissemination of controlled information are potent forms of deception, and the hyper-connectivity of the internet offers an easy conduit for falsehood.

The March 2017 Wikileaks dump of thousands of secret CIA documents revealed the agency's intrusive and illegal surveillance of private citizens in their homes and workplaces through remotely hacked smartphones, smart TVs and android gadgets; it disclosed the agency's ability to hack a target's car creating a 'malfunction' accident/assassination, as also their ability to leave a digital false flag implicating some uninvolved party, this last with international ramifications. The news anchor likened the stunning disclosure to an episode from the hit TV series *CSI Cyber* or its political-thriller rival, *Homeland*. After dodging the dump for days FBI Director James Comey finally addressed the privacy issue, admitting on March 8, 2017, 'There is no such thing as absolute privacy in America… even our memories aren't private.'

A bitter admission.

This, from the freest of all 'free' societies.

In 2013, Edward Snowdon the NSA whistleblower, also revealed an extensive illegal internet surveillance of ordinary American citizens under a data collection program called Prism, involving the servers of widely used companies like Facebook, Google and Apple. Ironically, the surveillance and spying-through-smart-gadgets claim was apparently made by alternative media over eight years ago but was dismissed as conspiracy theory.

We live in an Orwellian world.

By a strange coincidence, the timespan between the 33 A.D. crucifixion of Christ and the heavenly sign of 2017 is exactly 1984 years. This is the title of George Orwell's final work, written the year before his death, in which he coined the terms 'big brother,' 'thought police' and 'newspeak'; and that classic of twisted hypocrisy, the 'double-think,' words which have now passed into common usage. The novel presages restrictive, intrusive, untruthful government with institutionalised sectors of psychological manipulation which alter the character of a society. As the book was nearing completion Orwell wrote, 'I am inclined to call it *Nineteen Eighty-Four* or *The Last Man In Europe*, but I might just possibly think of something else in the next week or two.' [Orwell, personal correspondence, letter dated October 22, 1948].

Orwell kept his first selection but the reason he chose that particular year is unknown; some theorise it was an inversion of the year the book was completed, others link it to Chesterton's *The Napoleon of Notting Hill* – but no one knows for sure.

The work of two of Orwell's contemporaries is also deeply prescient. Aldous Huxley's futuristic novel, *Brave New World*, anticipates developments in reproductive technology, sleep learning and classic conditioning, using pleasure to control and an overabundance of the trivial to suffocate; his dystopic vision drifts into moral ambivalence. There is nothing ambivalent in H.G. Wells, author and ex-British Intel agent, whose writing embraced the future, even postulating a global brain, including the need for coercive propaganda and a socialist society. In 1928, Wells wrote, *Open Conspiracy: Blueprints for a World Revolution*; the book closely followed an earlier one, *Men Like Gods* – a title which echoes the serpent's promise, *ye shall be as gods…*

Let us continue with the types of deception.

Second on the list is something called 'wonders.'

Modern 'wonders' include swift travel and speedy knowledge. These are markers laid out by the angel Gabriel as he concludes the narration of his end-time plot, *But thou, O Daniel, shut up the words, and seal the book, even to the time of the end: many shall run to and fro, and knowledge shall be increased,* (Dan.12:4).

Knowledge shall be increased –

A prophecy fulfilled through the internet. Knowledge is now at our fingertips, no more than a click or tap away. In the recent past a phone did just that, phone someone. Now, with a Wi-Fi connect, it can take pictures, download information, scan the news, update your social media page, watch shows, play games, email, text and twitter; it can remind you of pending chores through Siri, direct you to your destination through GPS, or pay your bills, as needed.

Many shall run to and fro –

Truly, a prophecy of today. Never before have so many people in all walks of life, on a routine basis, run to and fro. We travel for pleasure, we travel for work, we cover great distances routinely without giving it a thought. Easy travel is a science/tech spinoff. For the longest time, for almost five thousand years – from the pharaohs of Egypt (c.3200 B.C.) to the post-Renaissance world of the 1700s – man's principal means of transport was the horse. But the 1800s saw a revolution in travel with the wondrous advent of the steam engine, Puffing Billy of the U.K., the 'iron horse' of the U.S. which opened up the West. The marvels of electricity passed into common use. Advancements followed: the car, the plane, jet engines, rockets to the moon, satellites and star probes.

The wonder of modern communication fulfils the prophecy of Matthew 24:14, *And the gospel of the kingdom shall be preached in all the world for a witness unto all nations; and then shall the end come.* The wonder of satellite TV would permit the two dead witnesses of God to be seen by all people, *And kindreds and tongues and nations shall see their dead bodies three days and an half*, (Rev.11:8-9).

How could all commerce be controlled so *no man might buy or sell* (Rev.13:17), but by the wonder of global interconnectivity? Or a two hundred million man army (Rev.9:16) be swiftly assembled but by the wonder of modern travel? Does the fifth vial poured over the seat of the beast rendering *his kingdom full of darkness* (Rev.16:10), suggest an EMP outage? Do the painful sores of *men scorched with great heat* (Rev.16:11), suggest radiation exposure?

The fulfilment – or potential fulfilment – of these prophecies is tied to a level of technology unimaginable at the time of its writing.

But present today.

Science/tech is an integral part of an allied form of 'wonder': amazement. The Apostle Paul, speaking of the antichrist, writes, *Even him, whose coming is after the working of Satan with all power and signs and lying wonders,* (2Thess.2:9).

The tech springboard has altered the reality of our world and also our notion of reality itself. Experiments in augmented reality, introduced playfully through game streaming and interactive devices, virtual reality immersion gear like Oculus Rift and HoloLens, and the magic of great spectacle, make 'wonders' easier to perform. The Billboard Music Awards, 2014, showcased the amazing on-stage resurrection of Michael Jackson in a 3D hologram. Holograms seemed a bold new frontier in the entertainment industry – but the envelope-pushing performer, Lady Gaga, made that wonder past tense at the 2016 Grammy's with her mind-bending tribute to David Bowie. Using the vehicle of computer graphics, interactive video and robotics, a digital 'skin' was projected onto the singer, so that her makeup changed instantaneously and her features seemed to morph during the live performance.

Full-environment 3D holograms are becoming, to use an oxymoron, routine wonders – like the dolphin splashing in the sea on a gymnasium floor in Dubai or the 'solid' hologram of a butterfly in Japan which offers the sensation of touch. But what about the ghostly city sitting on the waters of the Xin'An River near Huanshan, China, witnessed by hundreds of astonished passers-by and recorded on cell phones, in June 2011; the 'inter-dimensional' city floating over the village of Dulali, Nigeria, April 2015, also witnessed by hundreds; or the crowded skyscrapers hovering in the clouds above Guangdong, China, October 2015, witnessed by thousands and reported by local press – are these sightings a test balloon for counterfeit wonders? *Inquisitr*, a web magazine which reported the Guangdong event, gave the official version of refracted mirage; it also raised the possibility of Blue Beam.

Project Blue Beam refers to an exposé by Quebec investigative journalist Serge Monast (please google), on a covert NASA psy-op of that name, in 1996. Monast detailed a program of fabricated archaeological 'finds' causing man to question his origins, followed by immense astral 'wonders' on a sky-screen created by chemical seeding; these wonders would negate all religions by showing a progression of 'saviours', promoting the arrival of an ultimate (alien?) saviour and a single religion; these images would be accompanied by ELF (extra low frequency) vibrations which target the frontal cortex and pineal gland (third eye/knowledge), thus simulating a transcendental experience.

Unholy… (2Tim.3:2).

Inventors of evil things, (Rom.1:30).

For by thy sorceries were all nations deceived, (Rev.18:23).

The marvels of technology are speeding ahead, literally so. In November 2016, the UK *Mirror* reported on NASA's successful development of a warp drive engine based on electromagnetic propulsion, possibly drawing on Nikola Tesla's (once ridiculed) theory of an electric universe and plasma cosmology. A report, published nineteen months earlier, in April 2015 by *CNet*, had been originally denied by NASA. Warp drive opens yet more varied 'wonders'; does the 'fire from heaven' (Rev.13:13) link to the dynamic of ionised gases and plasma fields?

'Wonders' are a powerful deception, indeed.

A third prong of deception is tied to the curious sentence Jesus uses, *But as the days of Noe were, so shall also the coming of the Son of man be,* (Matt.24:37; Luke 17:26); *Likewise also as it was in the days of Lot; they did eat, they drank… Even thus shall it be in the day when the*

Son of man is revealed, (Luke 17:28-30).

What were the days of Noah like?

They were days of oblivion; men and women unmindful of the coming catastrophe, complacent, immersed in the pleasures of life. We may presume they ridiculed Noah as he laboured year after year on a massive boat built on dry land. Mockery and ridicule are part of the end-time scenario that the Apostle Peter references, *There shall come in the last days scoffers, walking after their own lusts, And saying, where is the promise of his coming?* (2 Peter 3:3-4).

Is there other information on the days of Noah?

Genesis 6:5 tells us that *the wickedness of man was great [and] every imagination of the thoughts of his heart was only evil continually* –

Every. Only. Continually. Evil.

The words underline an immense godlessness, *And it repented the LORD that he had made man on the earth... but Noah found grace,* (Gen.6:6-8).

God decides to start afresh. He chooses Noah, *a just man and perfect in his generations,* (Gen.6:9). The Hebrew word used for 'perfect' is 'tamim' (*Strong's Concordance* no.8549), which means perfect, without blemish.

Perfect, an odd word.

Perfect 'in his generations' (i.e. genetically pure) is even odder.

Seeking an explanation to this puzzle, Bible

scholars have uncovered suggestions – even direct statements in apocryphal texts – that are weirdly strange; but the strangeness of these suggestions are echoed by another strange verse in Genesis, one often bypassed in teaching, *That the sons of God saw the daughters of men that they were fair; and they took them wives of all which they chose,* (Gen.6:2).

[N.B. 'son of' in biblical parlance denotes a direct creation or direct descent; the Greek Septuagint renders this phrase 'Bene HaElohim' as 'angels of God', (see Charles Missler, *Learn the Bible in 24 Hours*); also see Jude 1:6, *The angels which kept not their first estate, but left their own habitation...*]

Dr. Michael Heiser, Bible scholar and Semitic languages expert, offers an explanation (his books, *The Unseen Realm*; also *Forbidden Union: The Legacy of Babel*) which has gained wide acceptance among scholars. It suggests a deliberate attempt to prevent the promise of salvation through the seed of woman and in the image of God by corrupting human DNA. The Flood largely wiped out this effort though pockets of corruption returned/survived: *There were giants in the earth in those days; and also after that,* (Gen.6:4). References may be found scattered through the Old Testament, as in, *And there we saw the giants, the sons of Anak, which were come of the giants: and we were in our own sight as grasshoppers, and so we were in their sight,* (Num.13:33).

Worth noting here: the Hebrew original of Genesis 6:4 uses the word 'nephilim' for giants, meaning 'fallen ones', drawn from the verb naphal, to fall (*Strong's Concordance* nos.5303; 5307).

A strange picture begins to emerge –

Did fallen angels try to mingle with man, altering human DNA? Did man-animal perversion create the hybrids of pre-Flood legend (the Minotaur of Crete, the centaurs of Pelion, the myth of Leda and the Swan, Europa and the bull)? And even if true, how could our days equal those days? Less than a hundred years ago this suggestion would have been science-fiction fantasy, beyond reality; but, in laboratories today, manipulated DNA is routine. Bioethical concerns have been raised about germline editing but restraints are loosening; the National Academy of Sciences recently softened its stance to permit cases where there are 'no reasonable alternatives,' [*New York Times*, Feb.14, 2017]. It opens a wide loophole, easing social acceptance of DNA alteration. CRISPR-Cas9 kits, available for the price of a good cell phone, permit genome editing, adding genes or snipping them off: the results are permanent, passed on to children; the mistakes are permanent too.

Three parent babies now exist.

Clones exist.

Animal hybrids exist: ligers and tigons, you have doubtless read about them.

And human-animal hybrids, they exist too;

created with wonderful intent.

Cross-species chimpanzee/baboon to man liver transplants and pig lung transplants have been performed (since the 1960s); hospital labs grow human ears on mice to facilitate acceptance during surgery (a photo released in 2006 created a public outcry); cows with human DNA have been successfully developed, producing almost-human breast milk (*Science*, Bovine Genome Sequencing, April 24, 2009); and human-pig hybrids (successful experimentation, *National Geographic*, January 26, 2017) could be the future hope of organ-donor lists.

Are we sailing for the Island of Dr. Moreau?

Science fiction and science fact have come together in our time. Recombinant DNA technology – or, more simply, DNA experimentation – has been recorded as far back as 2005, when the online issue *National Geographic News* reported on Chinese scientists injecting human cells into rabbit eggs and harvesting the stem cells of this strange chimera.

In July 2011, the *Daily Mail* online issue carried a report that over 150 human-animal hybrids were being grown in UK labs, with embryos secretively produced over at least three years.

In March 2013, *LifeNews.com* reported on a University of Rochester experiment in which nascent human glial cells from aborted embryos were implanted into newborn mice, helping the mice 'think.'

In May 2016, *NPR* ran an article on hybrid experiments conducted at the University of California and New York Medical College; Stuart Newman, professor of cell biology and anatomy at NYMC admitted, 'If you have pigs with partly human brains [they] might have human-type needs. We don't really know.' The moral and ethical issues raised by such controversial experiments are quietly sidelined.

In January 2017, Salk Institute for Biological Studies, California, recorded success in interspecies chimerism, with lead study author Jun Wu declaring, 'In ancient civilisations, chimeras were associated with God.'

Boasters...proud, unholy, (2Tim.3:2).

Incontinent, (2Tim.3:3).

And even as they did not like to retain God in their knowledge, God gave them over to a reprobate mind, (Rom.1:28).

Experiments in bioengineering, sanctioned by governments, are carried out by agencies like DARPA (U.S. Defense Advanced Research Projects Agency), who seek the creation of super soldiers – men who can grow back a limb, who can run with the speed of a leopard or see with the eyes of an eagle, what Annie Jacobsen (her book, *The Pentagon's Brain*) calls the incredible arena of military transhumanism. It is the X-Men in real life – like the UC Irvine Limb Regeneration center, funded by DARPA; or DARPA's

$32 million investment in synthetic DNA, an offshoot of the agency's Mammalian Genome Engineering Project, reported by *Tech Times*, Sept. 26, 2015.

Open news on these topics suggests the truth may be even further along.

On December 19, 2016, the Permanent Representative of Syria to the U.N., Bashar Ja'afari, declared before the Security Council, following adoption of U.N. Resolution 2328, that Syria was facing 'a genetically modified armed opposition, funded as moderates' by U.N. member states. This curious remark dovetails with remarks by U.S. Army Chief of Staff, General Mark Milley, to a gathering of ROTC cadets, that they would be required to deal with 'hybrid armies,' [Milley, speech at Norwich University, April 21, 2016]; a claim later watered down by an army spokesperson to mean a mix of conventional and non-conventional combatants – which hybrids would certainly be.

The definition of medical ethics has blurred and God has been removed from the equation. Francis Fukuyama, professor at John Hopkins SAIS and a member the President's Council on Bioethics, declared that transhumanism was 'a strange liberation movement' that sought to free the human race from its biological restraints, destroying the basis of equal human rights by destroying what Fukuyama termed 'the human essence.' He wrote, 'If we start transforming ourselves into something superior, what rights will these enhanced creatures claim, and what rights will they possess when compared with those left behind?' [Fukuyama, *The World's Most Dangerous Ideas*, 2004]. In 2006, McNamee and Edwards published a scholarly article in the prestigious *British Medical Journal* debating this same issue which is central to transhumanism, and detailing the slippery slope of 'quasi-medical ideology.'

Balancing these conservative views are men like Zoltan Istvan, candidate of the Transhumanist Party, or Nick Bostrom, Oxford philosopher and co-founder of the World Transhumanist Association, who declare an urgent need to improve on the 'half-baked' project that is man. The H+ premise envisions mankind transformed, with expanded abilities so beyond the natural condition as to merit the label 'posthuman', marking the rise of humanoids and human gods.

Professing themselves to be wise, they became fools, And changed the glory of the incorruptible God into an image made like to corruptible man… Wherefore God also gave them up to uncleanness through the lust of their own hearts, (Rom.1:22-24).

The quoted scripture underlines freewill.

The push for transhumanism has gone mainstream with the cover of the April 2017 *National Geographic*, 'The Next Human: Taking Evolution Into Our Own Hands'. *Homo Deus* is scheduled to become the next multibillion dollar industry.

Bioengineered plant and animal life, gene splicing, gene enhancement, memory editing and reprogrammed human beings are all on the agenda in this plan to deconstruct God's original design; and we have been familiarised with this subject thanks to a slew of movies in the last twenty years like *Gattaca, the Fly, Star Trek into Darkness, Jurassic Park, Watchers, Oblivion, Planet of the Apes, Edge of Tomorrow, Morgan* (to name a few).

Humanity 2.0 abandons Genesis 1:27 –

In the image of God created he him, (Gen.1:27).

Altered DNA may well be the mark of the beast.

In Daniel's vision of the king's dream, the iron mixed with miry clay is strangely linked to 'the seed of men'/human DNA and an unidentified 'they.' The exact passage reads, *And whereas thou sawest iron mixed with miry clay, they shall mingle themselves with the seed of men: but they shall not cleave one to another, even as iron is not mixed with clay,* (Dan.2:43).

Also relevant is Daniel's second vision of the four beasts from the sea, a composite of the end-time beast. The lion is made to stand on its hind feet and is given the heart of a man. This has been variously theorised by Bible scholars as representing the king's madness, as raising the lion to the status of a man, as lowering the lion by mocking its essential nature. These discussions all bypass the central idea of forced transformation, of becoming something else. Daniel's lion is an involuntary man-animal mix. Significant in this context is the winged lion itself; the winged lion was not a pervasive feature of Babylonian art but it appeared on the Ishtar gate, entrance to the city, and was the chief symbol of Ishtar, goddess of sex, including man-animal copulation (and presumably the results thereof).

Indeed, these activities are hinted at in the Bible. Separate reference may be found to men whose *faces were like the faces of lions,* (1Chr.12:8); and to *two lionlike men of Moab,* (2Sam. 23:20). The ancient kingdom of Moab runs north towards the prehistoric structure called Gilgal Refaim, which means 'wheel of giants' in Hebrew. Interestingly, this ring-shaped structure is called Rujm el-Hiri in Arabic, meaning means 'stone heap of the wild cat.' The very different descriptions identifying the same object offer a curious sidelight on truth.

The idea of transforming into something else also appears in the Bible story of Nimrod, that first builder who attempted the tower of Babel in the plain of Shinar. Nimrod is listed as the son of Cush (Cush, grandson of Noah). Genesis 10:8 declares that Nimrod *began to be a mighty one*; 'a mighty one', this phrase tied to the giants of Genesis 6:4 (also Deut.32:17; Num.13:33; Hebrew 'nephilim,' *Strong's Concordance* no.5303); 'began to be' suggests a method of transformation. The Hebrew word used here for 'begin' is 'chalal' (*Strong's*

Concordance no.2490), which carries connotations 'to defile, pollute, profane.' Whatever was attempted was a profanity not approved by God; both Nimrod and his tower were struck down.

[N.B. Compare the spirit of Nimrod/'chalal' with Noah/'tamim'; it provides a clearer idea of *the days of Noah* and the pervasive defilement of that time, substantially wiped out by the flood.]

Transformation is, in essence, the transhumanist agenda and it extends beyond man-animal manipulation to man-machine meld. This is equally the agenda of cyborgs and cosmists who see body hacking and bionics, brain uploads, implanted chips, wearable technology, life extension labs and cryonics as part of the future in a Brave New World; indeed, for a growing number of technophiles, the future has arrived thanks to rapid strides in advanced robotics and nanotechnology and 3D biological printers.

Can a wearable gadget make you think faster or even make you momentarily smarter? Apparently yes, if you use electrodes to shock your brain – which is how the Foc.us tDCS Headset (designed for gamers; transcranial Direct Current Stimulation) works, a device designed for short-term use by the gaming enthusiast. But can a similar device go mainstream?

Tech spin offs are spinning off at a dizzying pace.

Cutting edge innovations from different fields are coalescing.

Movies like *Transcendence* (2014), and *Lucy* (also 2014) have acquainted the less informed with the idea of a brain upload; we are familiar with Siri and the notion of self-driving cars, we are captivated by work surfaces that adjust to our needs and gadgets that respond to the command of our voice, we are ready for well-programmed robots who will assist us.

But are we ready for computer-brain interfaces and bio-bots?

Bio-bots are biological robots powered by muscle cells that have been genetically engineered with synthetic DNA; in this brave new world, AI (artificial intelligence) and AR (augmented reality) have finally fused man and machine into 'sentient' machines, a function of what may be termed programmable matter.

Having a form of godliness but denying the power thereof... (2Tim.3:5).

Incontinent, (2Tim.3:3).

Unholy, (2Tim.3:2).

A computer-brain interface links the brain to the computer. It can alter memory, upload information or download an instruction. This is not futuristic science tech, writes Paul McGuire in his latest book, *Mass Awakening*, but a developed and usable technology of today (albeit little known).

In December 2011, scientists working in collaboration with Boston University and A.T.R. Computational Neuroscience Laboratories in Kyoto,

Japan, published a paper on decoded neurofeedback or 'DecNef.' The process studied signals to the brain through a functional magnetic resonance imaging machine (FMRI), which can also alter brain activity patterns. Scientists believed that refinement of this new technology could enable the 'upload' of perceptual learning, i.e. imparting the knowledge of a musical instrument or a new language into a passive recipient. In August 2013, the *New York Times* carried a report, 'Computer-Brain Interfaces Making Big Leaps,' declaring that the science fiction world of brain tweaking had become real with a successful experiment by Riken-M.I.T. Center for Neural Circuit Genetics, creating a false 'memory' in a lab mouse.

The DecNef paper was released in 2011, the NYT report was 2013.

We are further down the road now.

We are talking neural lace.

Can technology destroy humanity?

Uploads and downloads link to the hive mind or global AI brain, plugging into a collective consciousness – but who will control this digital arena? The studies, doubtless done with positive intent, are open to easy misuse, opening a dark path of surveillance, mind control and technological singularity (presented as a thrilling positive in the journey of human consciousness in the new movie release, *Mindgamers*). But the hedonistic utopia anticipated by some may well be a virtual reality prison for all.

On March 1, 2017 *Popular Mechanics* announced the NUTM model developed by scientists at the University of Manchester, U.K., a near step towards their goal of a self-replicating DNA computer (following attempts on a biological supercomputer roughly the size of a book, reference Science Daily, February 26, 2016), replacing silicon chips with DNA molecules – but what will be the end role for man in this brave new world he is busy building?

The man-machine-AI construct, the fusing of the physical, digital and biological worlds is sometimes called 4IR or the Fourth Industrial Revolution. It is linked to IoT, the Internet of Things, a term coined by Peter Lewis in a 1985 speech to the U.S. FCC, foreseeing a world where everyday items would be embedded with electronics, software and internet connectivity.

It was then a thought; it is now a fact.

Human beings must merge with machinery to avoid irrelevance, this is the blunt message of futurists like Ray Kurzweil or Gray Scott who see 'a new technological species [with] the brain as a final frontier, we are looking at technology as a portal inward,' [Scott, *RT* interview, March 2017]; sometimes the bluntness is coated with ambiguity by men like Elon Musk, CEO of SpaceX and Tesla, who in a symposium at M.I.T., October 2014, acknowledged the fallout of AI as our 'biggest existential threat… we are summoning the demon' – this before announcing his computer-brain interface venture in March 2017, Neuralink, as the next step in human evolution. In April 2017, Mark Zuckerberg of Facebook confirmed rumours that his company was working on VR - AR software and a 'mind reading' brain interface, reference the *Daily Mail*, April 18, 2017.

AI is seeping into diverse aspects of common life.

On December 22, 2016, Apple published its first AI paper on marketing algorithms, a powerful new sales tactic in the offing. Coupled with plastic credit which tracks our purchasing habits and pop-up ads which track our interests, it is a fascinating new arena for the merchants of this world, an easy segue into the (Rev.13:15) scenario, *no man may buy or sell…*

On January 12, 2017, *The Guardian* published an article titled, 'Give Robots Personhood Status, EU Committee Argues'; it reports on a detailed draft submitted to the European Parliament, Commission on Civil Law Rules for Robotics.

On January 27, 2017, *ComputerWorld* suggested AI-based typing biometrics as an authentication tool of the future.

A dystopian comedy, indeed.

Remember iRobot, the Terminator and a dozen other techno thrillers? We are fully primed to accept AI in a servile capacity… though (a frisson of fear?)

we know that machines can and do run amok; but it is the future, the wonderful, unstoppable, progressive future. There is a label for this type of psychological messaging: it is called predictive programming; it promotes a feeling of hopeless inevitability.

GMOs were foisted on an unaware public.

So, too, the transhumanist experiment, begun in secret decades ago by a handful of scientists, is largely unknown to the common man whose life it will most impact. He may stumble upon some abstruse article which will inform him of the fact (unlikely, unless he is actively looking), or he will learn about it (in a fun way!) on the entertainment channel.

A cautionary note was struck by *Science Daily*, in an article February 23, 2017, carrying a source reference of University of Oxford, '[Bio-bots] appear to behave differently in culturally distinct online environments. Bots interact with one another, whether by design or not, and it leads to unpredictable consequences… the findings are a warning to those using AI for building autonomous vehicles, cyber security systems or managing social media.'

Kevin Kelly, co-founder of *Wired* magazine and author of *The Inevitable*, states that AI has arrived: 'It's here, it's real, it's quickening… and there's a spiritual dimension to [it].'

Fossbytes, a tech news magazine, writes February 21, 2017, 'AI machines are learning quantum physics and solving complex problems on their own.'

Actually solving? – through mimicry or through innovative thought? Apparently, the latter, part of deep learning algorithms being programmed into these machines.

Can AI become self-aware?

In a perceptive micro doc by Gonzo Shimura, March 1, 2017, titled, 'Is Artificial Intelligence the greatest threat to Christianity?', he discusses an article by Jonathan Merritt in *TheAtlantic.com* who equates the challenge of AI to Darwin's *Origin of Species* – who will the robot call God? Dismissed by many as a bit of high tech, the theological significance of AI is not fully understood and its ramifications could be extensive. Some deny the significance of AI declaring it does not appear in the Bible; but Shimura contends that the image of the beast (Rev.13:15) could well be a form of empowered AI.

AI: sentient, thinking; a sleeping giant more powerful than the men who created it.

AI, animated by synthetic human DNA –

Having a form of godliness, but denying the power thereof… (2 Tim.3:5).

Without natural affection… (2Tim.3:3).

Unholy, (2Tim.3:2).

It is Mary Shelley's *Frankenstein*, refashioned.

Corruption of some type is indicated in Gabriel's end-time plot in the Book of Daniel, in the contract between the king of the north and the king of south, one offering the other *the daughter of women, corrupting her*, (Dan.11:17). Historically, it was a marriage to secure Egypt (which failed); but the unusual language lends itself to a spiritual context, suggesting a treaty between nations on human seed/daughter of women; 'corrupting her' suggests defilement of this seed. Remember, a deep prophecy plays out very differently from the first enactment.

Will Armageddon be a genetic showdown?

The potential hazards of AI-AR are of our own making. And it falls in exactly with the serpent's lure, *ye shall be as gods*, (Gen.3:5).

Modern science appears to be on a collision course with God, starting with Darwin in the 1850s when God's role as Creator was first demeaned. If man wriggled as an amoeba out of the muck and by mutation and lucky chance succeeded in standing on his two hind feet – well, less glory to God! We cling to this theory even though the 'missing link' continues to stay missing after one hundred fifty years and even though the fossil record shows stasis with no transitional forms, a truth in stone which is conveniently bypassed. More importantly, twenty-first century advancements in the study of the human genome and the three-dimensional DNA code – its sequence and conformational shape as it is read – reveal transcription factors (TFs) linked in an incredibly complex system of interacting biochemical codes, unique to each species.

Studies show multiple codes within the same linear stretch of DNA sequences, accomplishing different functions. The inbuilt codes instruct on tandem repeats (TRs), telling genes precisely where to bind, and turning genes on and off; the satellite repeats originate from intergenic spacer of rDNA in complex eukaryotic genome, meaning that its smallest fundamental unit is a cell type which already contains specialised organelles in the cytoplasm, pre-programmed to a distinct function.

TFs and TRs mean that there is no such thing as one species 'evolving' into another.

There is no such thing as 'junk' RNA either, a pre-requisite of the evolution theory.

Darwin is dead, but no one will tell you; just sweep that embarrassing fact under the rug. As though anticipating the fallacy of Darwinian evolution, Genesis records the command that each living thing would bring forth abundantly *after their kind* (Gen.1:21), this exact phrase repeated not once or twice but six times over the next several verses on the creation and increase of life on earth.

Darwin is dead, but the damage he did lives on in philosophies like nihilism and atheism, political ideologies like communism, dangerous disciplines like eugenics and the rise of ambient technology which promotes the scientist as God.

In truth, the greater the scientist, the greater is his humility before God. Sir Isaac Newton (1642-1727), English physicist and mathematician, widely accepted as one of the most brilliant scientists of all time whose breakthrough discoveries on gravity, the laws of motion which underpin modern physics, optics and math (including the study of power series, the binominal theorem to non-integer exponents and calculus, including the empirical law of cooling, and his prediction that earth was an oblate spheroid, unknown at that time), discoveries which would define and shape all scientific development even till today, devoted a substantial part of his life to a study of the Bible. A 1936 historic auction of Newton's personal papers, conducted by Sotheby's, reveal Newton's overwhelming interest in the nature of God, chronology, the Apocalypse, Daniel's 70-week prophecy and an exhaustive examination of the measurements of Solomon's temple. Even the atheist Albert Einstein wrote, 'If something is in me which can be called religious, then it is the unbounded admiration for the structure of the world so far as our science can reveal it,' [Einstein, personal correspondence, letter dated March 24, 1954].

Man is the spiritual center of God's creation; spiritual, not physical. Our earth is one planet in the solar system; our sun is one of a few hundred billion stars that belong within our spiral galaxy, a tiny spec in a spur of the Orion Arm which is part of the

Milky Way; which itself belongs to a Local Group galaxy cluster; which is found within the larger Virgo Supercluster; which is, in its turn, a component of the super supercluster Laniakea.

And so on and so forth.

Wheels within wheels, to intrigue the intelligent; as a baby is stimulated by the mobile above his head; as a toddler reaches out to the object beyond the bars of his playpen. If we look at a scientific diagram of the Big Bang theory the picture that appears is of a sideways bell or megaphone/trumpet, *For he spake and it was done; he commanded and it stood fast*, (Psalm 33:9); science informs us that the universe is still expanding, as sound waves ripple out from a source, as a pebble thrown in the water creates expanding circles, as a bell vibrates.

But while the truly wise are humbled before the majesty of God's creation, the lesser are caught by imagined wisdom –

Because that, when they knew God, they glorified him not as God, neither were they thankful; but became vain in their imagination, and their foolish heart was darkened, (Rom.1:21).

Ever learning, and never able to come to a knowledge of the truth… (2.Tim.3:7).

Seduced by the serpent's power bait garnished anew for our time: eat, the serpent told Eve, *and ye shall be as gods…*

The 'as gods' philosophy predominates at CERN (French acronym, European Organisation for Nuclear Research), where particle physicists have attempted re-creating the Big Bang and are actively engaged in seeking parallel dimensions. Their work has been accelerated by the Adiabatic Quantum Computer, developed with D-Wave technology. Used in conjunction with the Large Hadron Collider, the ADQ is being employed to tunnel through to cosmic microwave background (please google the work of Anthony Patch). Sergio Bertolucci, head of Research and Scientific Computing at CERN, has been quoted as saying that, in their efforts at quantum tunnelling (equivalent to ripping the cosmic veil), they do not know 'what might come through.' This is an amazing statement. The dangers were highlighted by Steven Hawking who wrote that the Higgs Boson particle, unstable at very high levels of energy, could trigger 'a catastrophic vacuum decay which would cause space and time to collapse,' [Hawking, preface to *Starmus: 50 Years of Man in Space*, 2014].

It would seem that CERN is an end-time player.

In fact, there are several interesting aspects to CERN, starting with its logo of three interlocking 6s. Outside its headquarters in Switzerland is a large statue of Shiva in the dance of cosmic destruction and regeneration. Shiva is a Hindu god more frequently portrayed with a snake coiled about his neck, the mark of the third eye (illumination/knowledge) on his forehead and a thin crescent moon in his hair. A plaque beside this statue draws a correlation between ancient mythology, religious art and modern physics. Also interesting: part of CERN lies in the small town of Saint-Genus-Poilly, the old Roman city of Appolliacum; a temple to Apollo once stood here and local legend has it that Apollo will rise from this place in end times. Quite remarkable, when we remember Apollyon from Revelation (ch.9:11), king of the bottomless pit and the locust army, destined to rise when the fifth trumpet is blown.

Not surprisingly, the names and symbols of gods and goddesses from forgotten empires are resurfacing in our time on space probes, company logos and Hollywood sets, including esoteric images like the eye hovering above a pyramid which appears on the back of the U.S. one-dollar bill (first put into circulation in 1935). Though these ancient deities assumed different names in different empires, their symbols, primarily of the sun and moon, remained unchanged: thus in Egypt we find Ra and Isis; in Assyria: Ashur/Shamash and Ishtar/Astarte; in Babylon: Bel-Marduk, in triad worship with sun god Yarhibel and lunar god Aglibel; in Persia: Mithra and Allat; in Greece: Apollo and Artemis; in Rome: Sol and Diana.

Many of these gods and goddesses link to the Sun Seal religion of Mesopotamia with its 'magic' square of numbers 1-36, arranged so that whether computed horizontally or vertically the total arrived at would always be 666; this religion worshipped the sun, moon and select stars including Sirius and Alcyone (in Taurus) and the planet Saturn, discovered in the 1980s to have a peculiar and permanent wind-vortex hexagon on its north pole; some equate 666 with stars/angels controlled by the sun god (Rev. 9:1 draws a connection between a star and a fallen angel; thus 'stars' may be good or bad).

The pagan gods most frequently condemned in the Bible are Ba'al (also called Ba'alim, Bel, Belzephon, Beelzebub, Ba'alpeor) and Moloch (also called Molech, Marduk and Milcom) – gods worshipped by sexual excess and human sacrifice, particularly infanticide; the use of hallucinogenic or psychotropic substances to open 'portals' to these gods; and occult rites associated with the star Remphan/Saturn (Acts 7:43; Amos 5:26).

Are there parallels in our world today?

For men shall be lovers of their own selves…

Lovers of pleasures more than lovers of God… (2Tim.3:2-4).

Now the Spirit speaketh expressly, that in the latter times some shall depart from the faith, giving heed to seducing spirits and doctrines of devils, (1Tim.4:1).

For there are certain men crept in unawares, who were before of old ordained to this condemnation, ungodly men, turning the grace of our God into lasciviousness, (Jude 1:4).

Who changed the truth of God into a lie, and worshipped and served the creature more than the Creator, (Rom.1:25).

Oddly enough, the gateway to the temple of Bel, also called the Triumphal Arch of Palmyra, was re-created by the U.N. Institute for Digital Archeology (in collaboration with UNESCO and the U.A.E.) in an ill-chosen symbol of defiance against ISIS; it was unveiled in 2016-2017 in London, New York, Dubai and Florence. 2016 also saw the bizarre multimillion dollar opening ceremony of the Gotthard Base Tunnel in Switzerland, attended by powerful E.U. heads of state; a ceremony filled with transhuman images, principally the satyr (half man, half goat), symbol of the Baphomet. There is not only a falling away from God but a falling towards the dark supernatural with satanic cults and occultism on the rise in Europe and the U.S., promoted in the name of tolerance and protected by free speech and equal rights. Tracking parallel to this reversal is a new form of socialistic humanism but here, too, God is abandoned.

Something is stirring; the prophetic signs are all around us.

And the final sign? Convergence.

We are in that period which the Apostle Paul prophetically described as preceding the Second Coming, *For that day shall not come, except there come a falling away first, and that man of sin be revealed, the son of perdition; Who opposeth and exalteth himself above all that is called God, or that is worshipped; so that he as God sitteth in the temple of God, shewing himself that he is God,* (2Thess.2:3-4).

This know also, that in the last days perilous times shall come, (2Tim.3:1)

The end-time deception is of a magnitude so great that, were it possible, it might deceive even the elect (Matt.24:24); so overwhelming that the unaware will be caught in its web; so compelling that Christ warns, *when the Son of man cometh shall he find faith on the earth?* (Luke 18:8).

Keep not thou silence, O God: hold not thy peace, and be not still, O God. For, lo, thine enemies make a tumult: and they that hate thee have lifted up the head. They have taken crafty counsel against thy people… they are confederate against thee, (Psalm 83:1-5).

The ordinary man, the man in the street, is paralysed before this onslaught of evil as a bird is petrified into immobility before a snake as it slithers up to consume it.

Central in a psy-op battle is convincing the opponent of inevitability; there is nothing to be done, there is no point in resisting. Shock and awe. Succumb, it's hopeless. Written above the gates of Dante's hell are the words, 'Abandon all hope, ye who enter here.' [Dante, *Inferno*, Canto III].

Hopelessness is central to the Luciferian strategy but nothing is further from the truth. Satan, that most subtle serpent (Gen.3:1), is a liar and the father of lies, (John 8:44).

Take courage for we already know the end. The outcome is told us in advance; outlined in prophecy and validated by the past, thus –

Isaiah 46:1, *Bel boweth down.*

Jeremiah 51:44, *And I will punish Bel in Babylon… yea, the wall of Babylon shall fall.*

Hosea 2:17, *For I will take the names of Ba'alim out of her mouth.*

Judges 6:30, 8:21-28, *And [Gideon] cast down the altar of Ba'al and cut down the grove …[and] slew Zebah and Zalmunna and took away the ornaments that were on their camels' necks… thus was Midian subdued.* [N.B. Ornaments/'saharonim,' meaning 'little moons' of gold and silver in worship of Astarte, Gill's Exposition; also related to the Aramaic name for the moon god 'sahar,' Cambridge Bible (exegetical); Ellicott's Commentary; Benson Commentary.]

2 Kings 23:4-5, *And the king commanded Hilkiah, the high priest… to bring forth out of the temple of the LORD all the vessels that were made for Ba'al, and for the grove, and for all the host of heaven: and he burned them… And he put down the idolatrous priests… them*

also that burned incense unto Ba'al, to the sun, and to the moon, and to the planets, and to all the host of heaven.

The replacement of the Creator by his creation is part of the end-time game, where every 'game' has one goal: an attempt to divert or steal worship from God.

But victory belongs to Jesus.

We are told, *That at the name of Jesus every knee should bow, of things in heaven, and things in earth, and things under the earth: And that every tongue should confess that Jesus Christ is Lord, to the glory of God the Father,* (Phil.2:10-11); and again, *For it is written, As I live, saith the Lord, every knee shall bow to me, and every tongue shall confess to God. So then every one of us shall give account of himself to God,* (Rom.14:11-12).

A warning is issued to the people of God, *Babylon shall fall. My people, go ye out of the midst of her, and deliver ye every man his soul from the fierce anger of the Lord,* (Jer.51:44-45). This warning has a second witness, the wording almost identical, *And I heard another voice from heaven, saying, Come out of her, my people, that ye be not partakers of her sins, and that ye receive not of her plagues,* (Rev.18:4).

A warning is issued to pastors, preachers and priests, and those in instructive positions, also called the Watchman's Warning, *If the watchman see the sword come, and blow not the trumpet, and the people be not warned; if the sword come and take any person from among them, he is taken away in his iniquity; but his blood I will require at the watchman's hand,* (Eze.33:6). *Yet if thou warn the wicked, and he turn not from his wickedness, nor from his wicked way, he shall die in his iniquity: but thou hast delivered thy soul,* (Eze.3:19).

A warning is issued to the builders, *This is the stone which was set at naught of you builders, which is become the head of the corner. Neither is there salvation in any other: for there is none other name under heaven given among men, whereby we must be saved,* (Acts 4:11-12).

This is the stone which smote the feet of the statue in Daniel.

This is Jesus.

With the warning is an appeal, *Therefore also now, saith the LORD, turn ye even to me with all your heart, and with fasting, and with weeping, and with mourning: And rend your heart, and not your garments, and turn unto the LORD your God: for he is gracious and merciful, slow to anger, and of great kindness,* (Joel 2:12-13).

Let us return a final time to Daniel's statue. The feet of iron and clay are seen by some prophecy scholars as representative of the two forms of political government which will exist in end-time: the iron of totalitarianism, a hangover of the old autocratic regimes; and the clay of democracy, a new form of political government bending to the rule of ordinary man, the potter's clay.

The following off-the-beaten-path insight comes

ꜩ	50	נ	**Nun - Fish, Seed/Life, Continue**
Ħ	8	ח	**Chet - Fence, Wall, Separate**

Fig. xvi: Noah

from Australian pastor Steve Cioccolanti, citing the work of Hebrew scholar and pastor Mark Biltz. He posits the United States of America as the world's most powerful democracy, with the peaceful transition of power reflected in the office of the presidency. The U.S. is also the only democracy in the world with a fixed day for this transfer of power (since the 20th Amendment to the Constitution, ratified 1933): the twentieth of January of the year following an election year, held every fourth year.

The office of the presidency was established in 1789. The year 2017 thus marks the fifty-eighth presidential term of U.S. government; Donald Trump (45th president) entered the fifty-eighth presidential term of office.

Trump assumed office on 20-01-2017.

Counting in blocks of ten, this set of numbers also provides a value of 58.

In Hebrew numerics fifty is the letter 'nun'; it carries the meaning seed/life/fish/continue in pictogram; eight is the letter 'chet' meaning wall/separation. Quite remarkably, these two letters Nun-Chet form the Hebrew name 'Noah', (figure xvi).

The days of Noah –

Coincidence? Perhaps. Some say coincidence happens when we do not see the levers and pulleys and the little wheels that turn around.

Certainly, the ways of God are strange.

8 – Isaiah, the pyramid text

There is a text in Isaiah which reads, *In that day there shall be an altar to the LORD in the middle of the land of Egypt, and a pillar at the border thereof to the LORD. And it shall be for a sign and for a witness unto the LORD of hosts in the land of Egypt: for they shall cry unto the LORD because of the oppressors, and he shall send them a saviour, and a great one, and he shall deliver them,* (Isaiah 19:19-20).

A first reading of this passage seems to reference Exodus, when God (through Moses) led his people out of Egypt, guiding them as a pillar of cloud by day and a pillar of fire by night. But the prophet Isaiah wrote in the eighth century B.C., long after Moses and Exodus.

What pillar, then? What saviour?

What time period are we looking at?

Opening the same chapter, Isaiah mentions the Nile running dry: *And the river shall be wasted and dried up. And they shall turn the rivers far away,* (Isaiah 19:5-6).

The Nile has never run dry, not in known history.

But today the Nile *is* shrinking, slowly and steadily – not so slowly, in fact. And Isaiah's text provides both cause and consequence, in reverse.

In 2012, Ethiopia started work on a long pending hydroelectric project, a gravity dam ('they shall turn the rivers') built on the Blue Nile ('far away'), a rich source tributary which feeds the Nile. The Blue Nile originates in the mountains of Ethiopia, running north through Sudan where it joins the Nile and then onward to Egypt and the delta basin. The Grand Ethiopian Renaissance Dam, also called the Hidase Dam, is as yet unfinished but its effects can already be felt downriver, in Egypt, where the prophecy says, *the brooks of defence shall be emptied and dried up: the reeds and flags shall wither. The paper reeds by the brooks… and everything sown by the brooks, shall wither, be driven away and be no more,* (Isaiah 19:6-7).

Is Isaiah writing about the twenty-first century? The work of this prophet, writing eight hundred years before Christ, contains several Messianic passages sometimes called 'the suffering servant' prophecies; they look down the tunnel of the future to the passion and death of our saviour. Does this chapter look still deeper in time towards an even later event, the coming of a 'great saviour,' in victory?

Let us break up the prophecy into its parts.

What does 'in the middle' and 'at the border'

mean? Conflicting terms, surely. But this difficulty is soon solved. Ancient Egypt was divided into Upper and Lower Egypt, providing a 'middle'; the 'border' takes us to the Nile delta. It is a double identification which leads us to the Giza plateau and its chief claim to fame, the Great Pyramid.

The Great Pyramid is the only wonder of the ancient world that still endures. It stands 481.33 feet tall (minus its capstone which is missing); its base covers 13.3 acres; its individual stone blocks weigh between 3 and 30 tonnes; its estimated mass is 5.9 million tonnes; its volume is about 2.5 million cubic meters. The rough surface exposed to sightseers today was once covered by casing blocks of exceptionally hard limestone, a mantle of 1,44,000 blocks (computed from a small section which still covers the northeastern face), averaging 15 tonnes each. They were cut from the quarries of Tura and Masara, and polished to such brilliance that the pyramid shone like a mirror by day and was used to navigate craft on the Nile at night. In 1356, a major earthquake loosened many of these casing blocks which were scavenged and used in the building of many mosques in and around Cairo. The casing blocks still extant are placed to $1/200^{th}$ inch accuracy with an intentional $1/50^{th}$ inch gap for mortar. The mortar used by the pyramid builders has been taken and chemically analysed but cannot be reproduced.

Some of these statistics were chronicled by the

Egyptologist Sir Flinders Petrie in the mid-nineteenth century, but the marvels of this ancient structure grow with our growth in science and technology. The Pyramid builders are today acknowledged as architects and land surveyors, par excellence. The Great Pyramid stands at the northern extremity of a plateau overlooking the plain of Lower Egypt, simultaneously commanding the center of the Nile delta quadrant. It is built on a perfect north-south axis long before the compass was invented (the first compass dates back to the Han dynasty, China, in 206 B.C.; it appeared in Europe c.1300 A.D.); the Great Pyramid thus served as an immense sundial for ancient Egypt, marking the days and hours as also the equinoxes and seasons. Yet more amazing, the structure stands not only at the center of Egypt, but at a place that may be described as the center of the world (figure xvii).

Charles Piazzi Smyth, Royal Astronomer for Scotland, first recorded this discovery in 1864, declaring that the Great Pyramid was positioned at the geometric and barycenter of the total land mass of the world and arguing strongly for the earth's prime meridian to be shifted there. After years of exhaustive study, Smyth declared the Great Pyramid to be 'a perfect structure, a product of divine inspiration which embodied in its measurements a perfect system of weights and measures, among them the sacred cubit of the Israelites, the pyramid inch, and a system of prophecy.' [Smyth,

Our Inheritance in the Great Pyramid, 1864].

The Pyramid builders also show themselves as skilled geologists, well versed in natural physics, mathematicians of the highest order. In a sea of shifting sand, the Great Pyramid stands on solid bedrock, its foundation laid with such precision that, over the thirteen acres, the baseline does not vary by even ¼ of an inch. Heat expansion and seismic disturbance were provided for by engineering ball-and-socket joints into the granite bedrock at the four corners of the pyramid, securing the structure over natural calamity. Ventilation shafts within the pyramid use the principle of thermal dynamics to ward of deterioration, maintaining a constant and comfortable internal temperature of 20°C.

Twentieth century aerial photographs disclosed more wonders: a 'seam' running down the side of each

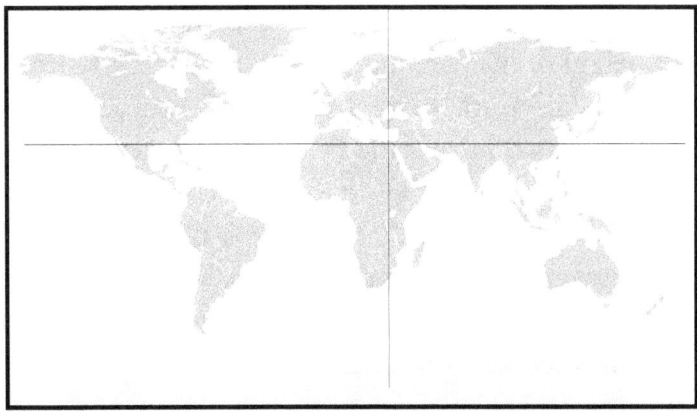

Fig. xvii: The Great Pyramid, barycenter of the planet's landmass

face of the pyramid, not visible from the ground, and visible from the air only under certain conditions of light and shadow. Examination of this seam reveals that each face is imperceptibly indented from base to top, working into the construction of this gigantic monument the principle of the arch, an incredible feat of engineering which has helped maintain the pyramid's integrity over time. Incredibly, this indentation is exactly proportionate to the curvature of the earth and executed with such an extraordinary degree of precision that the indentation cannot be noticed from any ground position or at any distance; it is only visible from the air and clearly perceptible only on the equinoxes.

Equally amazing is the 51°51'14" angle of elevation of the pyramid, precisely maintained. It results in a final structure that models the globe and simultaneously accomplishes the unique feat of 'squaring the circle' i.e. the height of the pyramid to its base is exactly twice *pi* (figure xviii). Kurt Mendelssohn in his book, *Riddle of the Pyramids*, compares the Pyramid construct to others from the Third, Fourth, Fifth Dynasty and subsequent dynasties; these pyramids have a typical slope of 43°30' to overcome construction problems. The odds of the 51°51'14" angle of slope of the Great Pyramid as a random selection are calculated by Mendelssohn at not less than 36000:1.

Science confirms the wonders that Flinders and

Smyth could only guess at a hundred years ago: the Great Pyramid not only reflects the earth in volume and area but also in weight, its estimated mass of 5.9 million tonnes is approximately one billionth of the estimated mass of earth; rising 10' to every 9', the pyramid slope gives a value of hx10^9, finely approximating earth's distance from the sun; its base measures 365.25 pyramid cubits, the length of a year; the mean altitude of the earth, first measured in the twentieth century, is identical to the height of the Great Pyramid (without capstone); in addition, the relationship between *pi* and *phi* (*phi*, a math symbol linked to the Fibonacci series) is an integral part of the Great Pyramid construct.

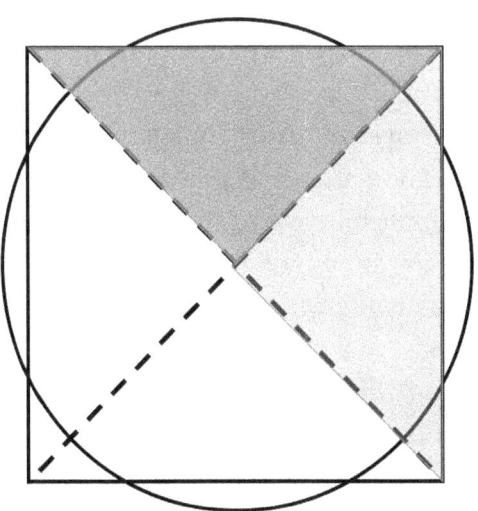

Fig. xviii: The Great Pyramid, squaring the circle, principle of pi

Let us leave these external marvels and travel to the mysteries within.

The Great Pyramid has been named after the Fourth Dynasty pharaoh, Khufu (2589-2566 B.C.; formerly Hellenised as Cheops). It is the only pyramid in the world constructed with a series of chambers and internal passageways. Once inside, we find none of the hieroglyphs that pervasively adorn all Egyptian monuments; there are no images offering worship to the gods, no praise of the ruling pharaoh, no record of achievement. The Great Pyramid, supposedly of the Fourth Dynasty, is in skill and accomplishment far beyond the pyramids of the Third Dynasty (now largely mounds of rubble) and those of the Fifth Dynasty (likewise). The Great Pyramid and its companion pyramids, Khafre and Menkaure, stand alone in grouped majesty, hugely superior in every aspect to the pyramids that came before and after – an astonishing anomaly, for there is no natural progression of architectural ability which marks a civilization; there is not even continuum of ability.

On what, then, does this attribution to Khufu rest?

William Fix in his book, *Pyramid Odyssey*, gives us an odd insight into the details presented to the world as fact. In a recess of one of the relieving chambers above the King's Chamber, along with some construction hieroglyphics, appears a small cartouche with the name 'Khufu' on it; in another relieving chamber, also with construction hieroglyphics, appears the name of 'Khnum-Khuf.' The dilemma of ownership was resolved because Khnum-Khuf was unheard of while Khufu's name appears on a monument in the Sinai. Close by the Khufu cartouche was a three-inch statue (of Khufu?), now on display in the Egyptian Museum, Cairo. It is on this three-inch pocket statue and an obscure cartouche in a relieving chamber that Khufu's claim to the Great Pyramid rests. Even the dating of this tiny statue has been challenged by many antiquities experts who date it to the Twenty-Sixth Dynasty (about 650 B.C.).

Compare this three-inch statue to the sixty-nine-foot tribute to Ramesses II at Abu Simbel or to the Sitting Colossi of Luxor or the towering statues of Karnak.

Compare the absence of inscription within the Great Pyramid to the hieroglyphic overflow in the Valley of the Kings or, indeed, of any commemorative monument in Egypt.

Most importantly, compare the absence of a body with any other Egyptian tomb.

Yes, this incredible pyramid was sealed off without Khufu (or anyone else) inside!

This astounding fact became known when Calif Al Mamoun, a ninth century governor of Cairo, had his men dynamite the massive granite slabs that sealed off the King's Chamber in his search for treasure, and found nothing but an empty stone coffer (similar to a sarcophagus but completely unadorned). This stone box was carved from a single block of red Aswan granite, so hard that diamond tipped drills with an overhead pressure of 1-2 tons would be required to replicate the precision and smoothness of its internal hollowing.

What Al Mamoun inadvertently proved by his dynamite and avarice was that the Great Pyramid had never been a tomb. In his disappointment, Al Mamoun missed another detail of the King's Chamber: the steeply climbing ventilating shafts drawing our attention to the stars. Only centuries later was this connection made, that the three pyramids Khufu, Khafre and Menkaure are precisely positioned to reflect the belt of Orion, slanted in a southwesterly direction, their orientation to the Nile reflecting that of the Orion belt stars Al-Nitak, Al-Nilam and Mintaka to the Milky Way; a terrestrial map of this star cluster.

Robert Bauval, in his book *The Orion Mystery*, charts this terrestrial reflection and follows it with a close examination of the three chambers of the Great Pyramid – the King's Chamber, impressive with its five relieving arches and flat roof of nine massive granite slabs arranged joist fashion; the smaller Queen's Chamber beneath with its vaulted ceiling; and dug deep in the bedrock an unfinished chamber with steep sides disappearing into rubble below (figure xix). Linking these chambers are the ascending and descending passage ways, ruler straight to within 0.013 inch per 100 ft., built at an angle of 26°18' 9".

The descending angle, taken north of east bisects the little town of Bethlehem; for this reason Bauval called it 'the Christ angle.'

On September 20, 2017, Al-Nitak (the first star of Orion's belt, matched on the terrestrial map by the Great Pyramid) will be at meridian, directly above

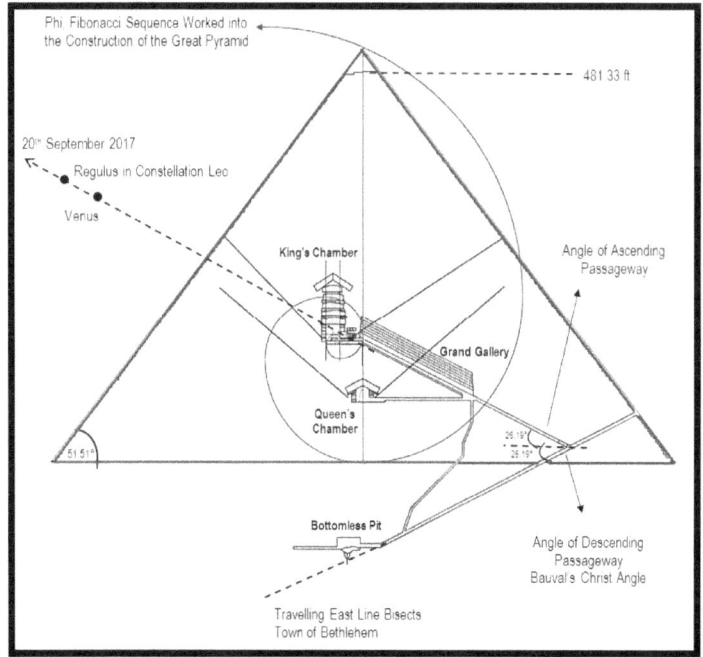

Fig. xix: Great Pyramid, the principle of phi, Bauval's Christ angle

the Great Pyramid; on this day, looking east, the 26°18' 9" Christ angle of the ascending passageway points directly to Regulus (the king star), in Leo (the king constellation), and bisecting Venus, a planet traditionally associated with the Jews.

Let us move briefly from the Great Pyramid to its guardian Sphinx: it is generally accepted that this colossal monument carved from a single limestone ridge had a lion's head to go with its body, subsequently fashioned (when the body was submerged in sand) into a pharaonic head. The sphinx looks east – does this enigmatic sculpture point to its constellation and a return date for the Lion of Judah (Rev.5:5)?

The Christ angle/Regulus alignment closely meets the 'woman in travail' date discussed earlier, heralding it. The convergence aids the theory that the Great Pyramid, in conjunction with its allied stars, functions as a 'moed,' fulfilling the pyramid text –

In that day there shall be an altar to the LORD... And it shall be for a sign and for a witness unto the LORD of hosts in the land of Egypt, (Isaiah 19:19-20).

If Khufu (most definitely) did not build the Great Pyramid, who did?

We do not know; but locals sometimes call it the pillar of Enoch. Who is Enoch? He is seventh in line from Adam (note the number seven), a pre-flood patriarch whose name means teaching or dedicated (see chapter 3). He is also one of only two men (the other is

Elijah) who did not die, according to the Bible, but was carried up to God, *And Enoch walked with God: and he was not; for God took him,* (Gen. 5:24). This statement is preceded and followed by the years of life granted to each of the other patriarchs, every lifespan ending with the words 'and he died' – except for Enoch.

The New Testament carries a validation of this man, *By faith was Enoch translated that he should not see death; and was not found, because God had translated him: for before his translation he had this testimony, that he pleased God,* (Hebrews 11:5).

Enoch is also referenced in Jude, in an apocalyptic passage of the last days, (Jude 1:14-23).

Enoch, the one whose name means dedicated to teaching, lived before the Flood. Is the Great Pyramid marked in any manner by water? Yes, there is a watermark around the base of the pyramid and water erosion marks the Sphinx at an equal level, congruent with such an event. Archaeologists who still try to tie the pyramid to Khufu are unable to explain water erosion in the dry, arid climate of the Giza plateau, an area that has minimal rainfall and has experienced no flooding in recorded history. Neither can they explain the salt incrustations, almost an inch thick, in the lower reaches of the pyramid. The salt encrustations decrease in thickness but continue all the way up the ascending passageway to the mid chamber, including the lower part of the Grand Gallery. They are consistent with sea water slowly abating and suggest a pre-Flood existence for the Great Pyramid.

[N.B. A note to those who are uncomfortable with the idea of a pyramid, considering it pagan – the proof, just cited above, places the Great Pyramid before the first recorded civilizations of early history; it is pre-historic; the power and majesty of this monument could explain why ancient Egyptians incorporated it into their religion (as modern occultism misuses the cross). Worth remembering in this context is the key of David, *And the key of the house of David will I lay upon his shoulder,* (Isaiah 22:22). The tetrahedron, delivered by the nail in the triangle, is a four sided triangle in space, as the Great Pyramid is a four sided triangle on earth; the pyramid image is also present in Daniel's stone which grows into a mighty mountain, a pyramid shape in nature.]

Enoch taught – and certainly the Great Pyramid has much to teach, lessons in stone. Multiple lessons, as we have seen. Lessons that may be understood only once we have already reached an understanding of subject – as the mysteries of the Shroud of Turin step up to meet each advancement of science, as the depth of math unfolds to meet the ability of the student.

Does modern confirmation of this ancient teaching held by the Great Pyramid suggest that it may contain further teaching beyond the physical and temporal?

Can the Great Pyramid have a spiritual message as Piazzi Smyth suggested?

In fact this is the conclusion of a section of Bible scholars who have examined the Great Pyramid in light of Isaiah's text. They see represented in the internal structure of chambers and passages – the only pyramid in the world to be so constructed – a mirror of the spiritual microcosm (see John Tatler's study of the pyramid inch, equating one inch to a year, *The Great Pyramid: Reflections in Time*; also Peter Lemesurier, *The Great Pyramid Decoded*).

These studies see the entrance passageway sloping downwards with a deeply scored groove in the wall as representing the fall of man; the ascending passage reflecting the Mosaic law; the start of the Grand Gallery marking the arrival of the Messiah; the King's chamber announcing the millennial kingdom; the strange chamber deep in the bedrock, rubble filled, with a deep pit at one end and a dead-end tunnel beyond, those who are doomed; the crooked path which falls away from the ascending passage to the bottomless pit, those who fall away from faith – or alternately those who try to struggle back up.

From within to without – to the limestone casing blocks that once cloaked the pyramid. Computing from those which still cover part of the northeastern face, researchers have determined the original total as 1,44,000 blocks. It is a number straight from Revelation.

The polished casing blocks represent those chosen from the twelve tribes of Jacob (Rev.7:4); they will ride with Jesus Christ into spiritual battle (Rev.14:1), spreading the mantle of His Word over the world during the last days.

And finally, to the top of the pyramid.

The Great Pyramid is without a capstone. There is a complete absence of mortar on the upper surface, suggesting it was never laid. This odd detail appears to validate the spiritual reflection-in-miniature theory – as Jesus was the cornerstone (the first coming), so he is also the capstone (the second coming); the capstone will only be fitted when Jesus returns in glory on the last day.

In that day there shall be an altar to the LORD…

Does the Great Pyramid of Giza hold further information? As its exact dimensions reflect the world we live in, as its internal passageways reflect man's spiritual journey, do the external measurements hold significance too?

This is the argument made by David Flynn in his brilliant, sometimes esoteric book, *Temple at the Center of Time: Newton's Bible Codex Finally Deciphered*. Using the unified field theory first proposed by Sir Isaac Newton, and building on Newton's preoccupation with the measurements of Solomon's Temple, Flynn uncovered a space-time continuum linking the Temple Mount to key events in Israel's history; as example the distance between Babylon and the Temple Mount is 539 miles, in 539 B.C. Cyrus' victory marked Jewish freedom; the distance between the London Stone (established by the Romans as the point of measurement for Britain), and the Temple Mount is 1948 miles, in 1948 A.D. Israel was reborn and Britain was a key player in this event. These examples, among others, show the Temple Mount as a timepiece for events impacting Jerusalem. Flynn theorises a connection between the first altar to the Lord (Solomon's Temple) and the last (the Great Pyramid), worked as below:

The height of the Great Pyramid is 481.33'

Since the Great Pyramid has accomplished the unique feat of 'squaring the circle,' the height doubled gives the value of its diameter, 481.33 x 2 = 962.66'

Flynn proposes 962 B.C. as the year when Solomon's temple was dedicated.

[N.B. There is no exact year for this event, only approximations. Jewish records place the dedication of the First Temple in the eleventh year of Solomon's reign but there is no definitive date for when Solomon's reign commenced; 962 B.C. is within the accepted timeframe of Solomon's reign.]

962.66 x pi = 3024.28' perimeter of pyramid

Transposed as years –

3024.28 biblical years = 2980.8 solar years

Travelling forward –

962 B.C. + 2980.8 years = 2019.8 (adjusting for no year 0), say 2020 A.D.

The result of these calculations is interesting.

The number 2980.8 – did you recognise it? We met those digits as a whole figure in the first chapter of this book; it is the distance from the Temple Mount to Bethlehem. In a space-time fourth dimension paradigm, what appears to be encoded in the equation is the space/location of Jesus's birth in his first coming and the time/year of his second coming, (within Tribulation, Rev.14:1; or at the end of it, Rev.19:11).

2980 has one other significance: there is only one verse in the entire bible (both Old and New Testament) with a numeric value of 2980; this one, *So David gave to Ornan for the place six hundred shekels of gold by weight*, (1Chr.21:25).

It is David's purchase of the threshing floor.

It is here in Mount Moriah, the holy mountain of God (where Abraham had once been called to offer sacrifice), that David built an altar and offered sacrifice for God's mercy. This is where David instructed for the temple of God to be built and where his son, Solomon, carried out his wishes; commencing the building in the sixth year of his reign and completing it in the eleventh, the First Temple to the Lord –

Then Solomon began to build the house of the LORD at Jerusalem, in Mount Moriah, where the LORD appeared unto David his father, in the place that David had prepared in the threshing floor of Ornan the Jebusite, (2Chr.3:1).

The threshing floor is typically a place where wheat is separated from the chaff. The image appears often in the Old Testament but only once in the New, in a prophecy of John the Baptist recorded in Matthew; *but he that cometh after me is mightier than I, whose shoes I am not worthy to bear… whose fan is in his hand, and he will thoroughly purge his floor, and gather his wheat into the garner; but he will burn up the chaff with unquenchable fire,* (Matt.3:11-12).

The winnowing fan, used in threshing.

The garner, a barn for storing grain.

The tribulation, a period during which *many shall be purified, and made white, and tried: but the wicked shall do wickedly: and none of the wicked shall understand,* (Dan.12:10).

Once again we find ourselves at the door of a zone.

9 – 2017, a marker

There is a school of thought which decries the study of prophecy, especially end-time prophecy (which is all we have left), as examining a subject we should not approach. That Christ has come, that he will come again – it is enough; did not Christ say that the last day was known to *no man, no, not the angels of heaven, but my Father only,* (Matt.24:36)?

Indisputably, he did.

Should we then turn away from prophecy?

But then again, who is prophecy for?

A refusal of prophecy disregards the very reason and purpose of prophecy. It disregards the warning voice of God. God speaks through prophecy using his messengers, the prophets; and the prophets never carry a hey-you're-doing-great message; they carry advice to be heeded.

Prophecy cautions and it can counsel.

For this reason the study of prophecy can safeguard one's soul.

While Christ informs us that we may not know the day or hour in exact knowledge (precisely), yet we are required to know the framework (an approximation). The need for such knowledge is made abundantly clear by Christ himself. In Luke, Jesus directly rebukes the people of Jerusalem for not knowing the day (approximate) of their Messiah –

And when he was come near, he beheld the city, and wept over it, Saying, If thou hadst known, even thou, at least in this thy day, the things which belong unto thy peace!... For the days shall come upon thee that thy enemies shall cast a trench about thee... because thou knewest not the time of thy visitation, (Luke 19:41-44).

This rebuke also appears in Jeremiah, *The stork in the heaven knoweth her appointed times; and the turtle and the crane and the swallow observe the time of their coming; but my people know not the judgement of the LORD,* (Jer.8:7)

And in Hosea, *My people are destroyed for lack of knowledge,* (Hosea 4:6).

This same idea imbues the Apostle Paul's letter to Timothy, *Study to shew thyself approved unto God, a workman that needeth not to be ashamed, rightly dividing the word of truth,* (2Tim.2:15).

We may not know the day or hour but we are required to know the season.

Indeed, we are commanded to *watch*.

The command to watch appears in Matthew,

Watch therefore: for ye know not what hour your Lord doth come, (Matt.24:42).

In Mark, *Watch ye therefore for ye know not when the master of the house cometh… And what I say unto you I say unto all, Watch,* (Mark 13:35-37).

In Luke, *For as a snare shall it come upon all them that dwell on the face of the whole earth. Watch ye therefore, and pray always,* (Luke 21:35-36).

And in Revelation, *Behold, I come as a thief. Blessed is he that watcheth,* (Rev.16:15).

The need to watch is a prophetic warning.

This book has approached end-time prophecy through a varied and disparate lens: through names, numerics and ancient feasts; through history and math; through vision, parable and pictogram; through overt symbol and hidden cipher.

And now, through markers.

Calendar markers in countdown mode.

The years listed below mark events that impacted either the Church or Israel, anniversaries both ecclesiastic and secular. They also mark timespans laid out in the Bible as prophetically significant: the one-hundred-twenty-year span of Genesis 6:3; the fifty-year jubilee, Leviticus 25:10 (and multiples thereof); the notion of generation (as a multiple of seven, the number of completion and rest); three (multiples thereof); seventeen (to be explained).

Seven markers if we look at a narrow timeframe;

one more, if we expand our view. I will list all eight here, as under:

- 1517 = 500 years, the capture of Jerusalem by the Ottoman Turks (Jan.1517); the Reformation (Oct.1517)
- 1897 = 120 years, the First Zionist Congress, petitioning a Jewish state (Aug.1897)
- 1917 = 100 years, Our Lady of Fatima, six apparitions (May-Oct.1917); Russian Tsar Nicholas II abdicates, Lenin introduces communism (Oct.1917); General Allenby takes Jerusalem on foot, without bloodshed, and Britain draws up the Balfour Declaration, laying out a Jewish state in Palestine now under British mandate following fall of the Ottoman Empire (Nov.1917)
- 1947 = 70 years, U.N. Resolution 181(II), partition plan of Palestine, accepting the Balfour Declaration and authorising the creation of Israel (Nov.1947)
- 1967 = 50 years, the Six-Day War and capture of East Jerusalem (June 1967)
- 1987 = 30 years, First Intifada (Dec.1987, lasted seven years, ends with Oslo Peace Accord)
- 2000 = 17 years, Second Intifada begins; the Israeli Knesset commissions a separation barrier; the Wall of Gabriel's prophecy is fulfilled (Sept. 2000)

- 2017, year of countdown – *And there appeared a great wonder in heaven, a woman clothed with the sun, and the moon under her feet and upon her head a crown of twelve stars: And she being with child cried, travailing in birth and pained to be delivered…* (Rev.12:1-2).

Technology, through the Stellarium app, has permitted us the advance identification of a rare once-only alignment in the heavens (already discussed), a star map meeting all the criteria of this verse.

It occurs on September 23, 2017.

Tracking through thousands of years of star history, prophecy watchers have determined that the exact and perfect representation of this sign occurs only once, on the day cited above. But their search turned up a curious find. An imperfect copy of this configuration occurred once before; also just once. In this imperfect copy (presented in the work of Jaco Prinsloo), Jupiter strays outside the 'womb' of the constellation (as an active baby may kick stretching its mother's stomach?), before returning back to the womb. But the period of straying totals ninety-nine days, an excessive absence, and therefore dismissed as untenable and invalid.

This once-only imperfect copy is, however, the closest match to the once-only sign of Revelation 12.

Does this poor copy hold meaning?

What can it tell us?

It occurred on August 5, 3915 B.C.

3915 B.C. to 2017 A.D. = 5931 solar years (adj. for no year 0) = 6017 biblical years

What is the significance of this calculation?

And the LORD said, My spirit shall not always strive with man, for that he also is flesh: yet his days shall be an hundred and twenty years, (Gen.6:3). This lays out a prophetic six thousand years, the allotment of man. Can this blurred copy from 3915 B.C. mark Adam's fall into sin, does the passage of six thousand years mark the end of this assigned period?

But, to be precise, we have passed 6000 years.

Why 6017, does 17 have special meaning?

Let us examine some possibilities, starting with the final miracle of Christ, the stupendous catch of fish that is recounted at the end of John's gospel.

[N.B. A similar miracle marks the start of Christ's ministry in which a barren night of fishing ends in a catch that fills the boats to tipping point; Christ speaks to a kneeling Peter, *Fear not; from henceforth thou shalt catch men,* (Luke 5:10).]

The final miracle occurs after the resurrection. Once again Peter and some disciples have gone fishing; once again it is a night without success. As they return in the early dawn, exhausted with failure, a man on the shore orders them to cast their net to the right of the boat. They are rewarded with a huge catch, *great fishes, an hundred and fifty and three: and for all there were so many, yet was not the net broken,* (John 21:11).

And, with the miracle, Jesus is recognised.

Joyfully, his disciples scramble to the shore dragging their huge catch and Christ prepares breakfast for them, fish and bread, broiled on hot coals. The meal suggests fellowship and physical nourishment that Jesus provides equally with spiritual sustenance; the miracle declares his ability to turn nothingness to plenty, with trust and implicit obedience. But what does 153 mean – it is a number that has long been wrestled with, the only time it occurs in the Bible.

The seventeenth triangular number is 153.

17 is also the seventh prime number, (7, the number of completion).

Ezra, who kick-started Daniel's Seventy-Weeks Prophecy to the first coming of Jesus Christ, was seventeenth in line from the first high priest, Aaron.

June 17, 2 B.C. Jupiter and Venus stack together in the night sky, 36 arc seconds apart, coalescing into a star of immense brilliance as has not been seen before or since, hanging low in the night sky over Judea.

17 ties our world to the cross. Till less than a hundred years ago man comfortably believed in a 3D world, perfectly represented in math by a cube; but in the twentieth century, time (or space-time) was added as a fourth dimension. String theory adds other 'furled,' unknowable dimensions, but only these four are knowable. Oddly enough the Apostle Paul

identified four dimensions in a letter to the Ephesians, two thousand years ago –

That Christ may dwell in your hearts by faith; that ye being rooted and grounded in love, May be able to comprehend with all saints what is the breadth, and length, and depth and height; And to know the love of Christ which passeth knowledge, (Eph.3:13-19).

The text binds the four dimensions to God's love.

The 4D analog of a cube is called a tesseract (figure xx). Just as the surface of a regular cube has six square faces and can unfold into a 2D cross, so the hypersurface of a tesseract has eight cubical cells and 24 faces. A tesseract cut along 17 faces unfolds into a 3D cross – look up the image gallery on a math site; the animated tesseract and 3D cross are powerfully 'alive.'

Nisan 17, Jesus rose from the dead.

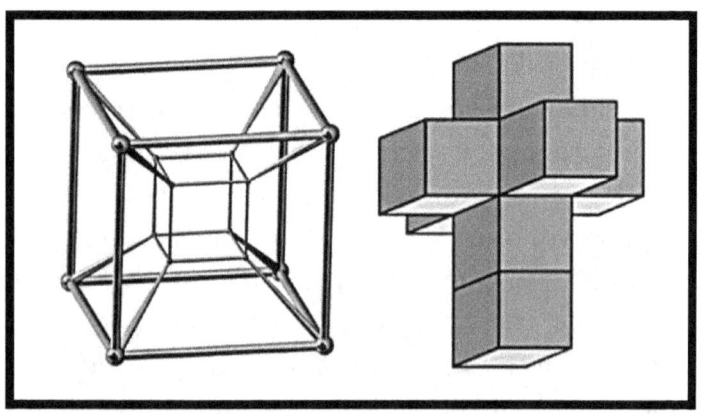

Fig. xx: Tesseract, 3D Cross

On the seventeenth day of the second month Noah's ark rose on the flood waters, (Gen.7:11); on the seventeenth day of the seventh month the ark rested upon the mountains of Ararat, (Gen.8:4); both acts demonstrate God's saving power.

Counting from the days provided in the Bible (Exo.3:18; 5:3; 14:1-22), the Israelites are three days from the first Passover, in their flight from Egypt, when they are pursued by Pharaoh's troops and Moses parts the Red Sea, Nisan 17.

Nisan 17, king Hezekiah cleanses the Temple after the corruption of Ahaz (2Chr.29:17-20).

Interestingly, the little village of Modi'in lies 17 miles from Old Jerusalem (spatial distance from the Temple Mount linked with temporal significance, already discussed). It was here that the local rabbi Mattathias refused the orders of the Seleucid officials and began the Maccabean revolt.

17 years from the countdown date marks the building of the Wall, the final piece of the Seventy-Weeks Prophecy laid out in the Book of Daniel.

On an odd little side note, the seventeenth letter of the old Greek alphabet was *pi* (the original alphabet contained three letters now obsolete, one of which was *digamma*, the sixth letter); *pi* x 10^{17} gives us the value of the first verse in the Bible, the creation verse of Genesis, *In the beginning God created the heaven and the earth*, (Gen.1:1).

17 also offers delay.

The image of delay occurs repeatedly in scripture as a time of testing.

Thus, in Exodus, *And when the people saw that Moses delayed to come down out of the mount, the people gathered themselves together unto Aaron, and said unto him, Up, make us gods which shall go before us; for as for this Moses, the man that brought us up out of the land of Egypt, we wot not what is become of him. And Aaron said unto them, Break off the golden earrings… and bring them unto me,* (Exo.32:1-2). In this excerpt, though the greatness of Moses is experienced personally by the Israelites, in the immediate past, yet the wait proves too long.

In Luke we are again presented with delay, *Blessed are those servants, whom the Lord when he cometh shall find watching: verily I say unto you, that he shall gird himself, and make them to sit down to meat, and will come forth and serve them. And if he shall come in the second watch or in the third watch, and find them so, blessed are those servants,* (Luke 12:37-38). This blessing is followed by a warning for the unjust servant who abuses his power and the sleeping householder who awakes to find his home broken into and his goods taken.

Delayed justice is the theme of the 'wheat and tares' parable, *The kingdom of heaven is likened unto a man which soweth good seed in his field: But while men slept, his enemy came and sowed tares among the wheat,*

(Matt.13:30). The servants suggest pulling up the tares; but this action will damage the good seedlings too and the owner decides to wait until the harvest; then the tares will be gathered and burnt, but the wheat is taken into his barns.

A final image of delay is the end-time parable of the ten virgins. The virgins are dressed, waiting for the bridegroom and the wedding feast, but the bridegroom is late. They fall asleep, waking up to the shout of his coming – but only five have oil enough in their lamps to accompany him into the wedding hall. When the foolish virgins eventually return with their lamps full, the banquet door is locked. They cry out, *Lord, Lord, open to us. But he answered and said, Verily I say unto you, I know you not. Watch therefore, for ye know neither the day nor the hour wherein the Son of man cometh*, (Matt.25:11-13).

Delay is a declared part of the 'last days' setup.

Delay ensures that we 'do not know the day or the hour;' this knowledge is for God alone.

Delay and the need to watch go hand in hand.

To watch for what?

To watch and recognise the end-time plot laid out in Revelation; to watch and guard against a season of deceit when deception will look like reality and reality like deception; a version of The Matrix, in real time –

Woe unto them that call evil good and good evil; that put darkness for light and light for darkness; that put bitter for sweet and sweet for bitter! Woe unto them that are wise in their own eyes...Which justify the wicked for reward, (Isaiah 5:20-23).

Who changed the truth of God into a lie, and worshipped and served the creature more than the Creator, (Rom.1:25).

I will lay out a final timeline.

This timeline was delivered by our saviour himself.

To place this event chronologically in the life of Jesus we must return to the Olivet discourse: Jesus is preparing his disciples for his near departure; we can feel their fear, we hear their anxious question, *what will be the sign of thy coming?* Jesus lays out a series of markers which he calls the beginning of sorrows (Matt.24:8); he follows it with a description of great tribulation marked by great deceit (Matt.24:15-29); he ends with the sign of the Son of man and the gathering of the Elect, (Matt.24:30-31). Unlocking these events is the parable of the fig tree –

Now learn a parable of the fig tree; when his branch is yet tender, and putteth forth leaves, ye know that summer is nigh: So likewise ye, when ye shall see all these things, know that it is near, even at the doors. Verily I say unto you, This generation shall not pass till all these things be fulfilled, (Matt.24:32-34; Mark 13:28-30; Luke 21:29-32).

The parable of the fig tree is recorded in all three synoptic gospels.

In all three texts, it is placed with Christ's Olivet discourse on end times.

In all three texts the parable of the fig tree opens with a command to 'learn' or 'know' and concludes with the words, *Heaven and earth shall pass away but my words shall not pass away,* (Matt.24:35; Mark 13:31; Luke21:33).

The parable of the fig tree appears after Christ's description of the great tribulation but it signals the start of tribulation. It will be remembered that in the Seventy-Weeks Prophecy (Dan.9:24-27), the consequence appears in verse three but the trigger event is delivered in verse four; the second set of numbers ties in with the first coming, the first set with the second; so also, in Isaiah's prophecy on the Nile, the consequence appears in verse five, the trigger in verse six (Isaiah 18:5-6). This contrapuntal delivery of prophecy identifies the timeline prophecies.

With this in mind, let us look at the parable of the fig tree which we are required to 'learn.'

The 'fig tree' is a metaphor for Israel.

Israel is frequently pictured as a fig tree or the fruit thereof in the Old Testament: thus, in Jeremiah, Israel is called a 'basket of figs,' *One basket had very good figs, even like the figs that are first ripe: and the other basket had very naughty figs, which could not be eaten, they were so bad,* (Jer.24:2; this precedes the judgement of captivity in Babylon); the fig image also appears in

Hosea, *I found Israel like grapes in the wilderness; I saw your fathers as the firstripe in the fig tree at her first time*, (Hosea 9:10).

The withered fig tree appears in the gospel of Mark, in the period between the joyous welcome of Palm Sunday and Christ's crucifixion. Jesus is staying in Bethany, home of Lazarus and his sisters Mary and Martha (it is Mary who anoints the feet of Jesus, John 11:1-2). Bethany is situated east of the old city of Jerusalem, on a winding road which curves around the base of the Mount of Olives, about a two mile walk from the city gates. The approach road offers a clear view of the city and temple; it is on this road that Luke records Jesus's tears, his rebuke of Jerusalem and his prophecy on the city and Temple, fulfilled in 70 A.D., *And [they] shall lay thee even with the ground, and thy children within thee; and they shall not leave in thee one stone upon another; because thou knewest not the time of thy visitation*, (Luke 20:44).

Along this curving road between Bethany and Jerusalem is the fig tree of Mark's gospel.

The fig tree is in leaf; Jesus is hungry and seeks fruit on the tree; he finds none, *for the time of figs was not yet. And Jesus [said], No man eat fruit of thee hereafter for ever... And in the morning as they passed by, they saw the fig tree dried up from the roots*, (Mark 11:13-14, 20; also Matt.21:18-20).

This incident is sometimes presented as a bizarre

example of faith-testing, sometimes used to show Christ as man in a too-human, petulant response; but it is neither. The incident is an acted-out parable.

A fruitful fig tree will put out breba or taqsh, just before or simultaneously with its first leaves; breba grow off the old stem, edible but with a tough skin, inferior to the sweet figs which will come off new growth in the summer (figure xxi). A fig tree with no breba will bear no fruit. Common breba are green or greenish-brown; therefore Jesus seeks first before speaking. In this dramatized parable, the breba represents true religion, the leaves empty ritual; the withered tree is consequence. It is noteworthy that Jesus speaks directly to the fig tree, condemning it. In the gospel story Jesus walks on to Jerusalem and the temple where he clears out the money changers.

The gospel of Luke records one more parable of a fig tree, that of a man who planted a fig tree in

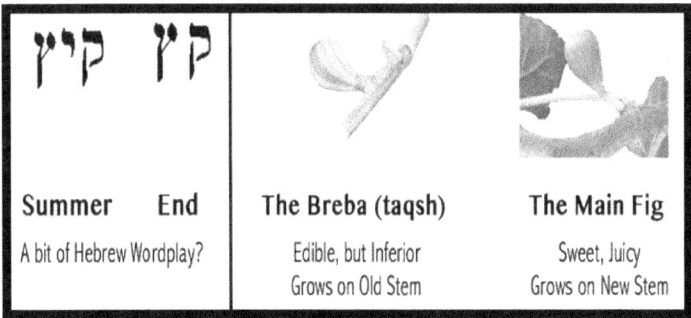

Fig. xxi: The fig tree parables explained

his vineyard and searched for fruit on it for three years without finding any. He orders it cut down but the gardener pleads for time *to dig about it and dung it, And if it bear fruit, well: and if not, then after that thou shalt cut it down,* (Luke 13:8-9). The three years in this parable reference Christ's ministry on earth (while some accepted his word, the 'barren' leadership did not); some see the digging and manure as the time in which the Apostle Peter preached God's word to the Jewish people; others equate it with the period between the crucifixion and the second coming, a final chance before judgement.

Returning to Jesus's end-time parable, the 'tender branch' is fresh growth.

It points directly to Israel's rebirth, May 1948.

The dispersal and regathering of the Jewish people is prophesized in the Old Testament (note the eschatological-apocalyptic manner of address), *Son of Man, when the house of Israel dwelt in their own land, they defiled it by their own way and by their doings… And I scattered them among the heathen, and they were dispersed through the countries: according to their way and according to their doings I judged them… But I had pity for mine holy name [and] I will sanctify my great name… For I will take you from among the heathen, and gather you out of all the countries, and will bring you into your own land… Then will I sprinkle clean water upon you, and ye shall be clean,* (Eze.36:17-35; also Deut.30:5-6).

Significantly, artistic representations of the constellation Virgo (virgo=virgin; virga=tender shoot or twig), traditionally linked to the affairs of Israel, always show a woman with a branch in her right hand. Christ's words hold verbal juxtaposition for the Jewish people: 'summer' and 'end' in Hebrew are very similar in script and phonetics (figure xxi); this wordplay also surfaces in a similar text from the prophet Amos, *And he said, Amos, what seest thou? And I said, A basket of summer fruit. Then said the LORD unto me, The end is come upon my people of Israel; I will not again pass by them anymore,* (Amos 8:2). The summer fruit of ancient Israel was typically figs; 'summer' and 'end' are explicitly tied in this passage.

And so to the end of Christ's prophecy, the promise: 'this generation shall not pass.'

When Israel became a nation, the last generation began.

How long is a generation? The Bible tells us, *The days of our years are threescore years and ten; and if by reason of strength they be fourscore years, yet is their strength labour and sorrow; for it is soon cut off, and we fly away,* (Psalm 90:10).

Seventy years, on the outside eighty.

Seventy years from Israel's rebirth in 1948 brings us to 2018 (2017, if we count from the U.N. decree in 1947, the prophet Daniel's 'going forth of the command'). An eighty-year generation takes us to

262 | END ZONE

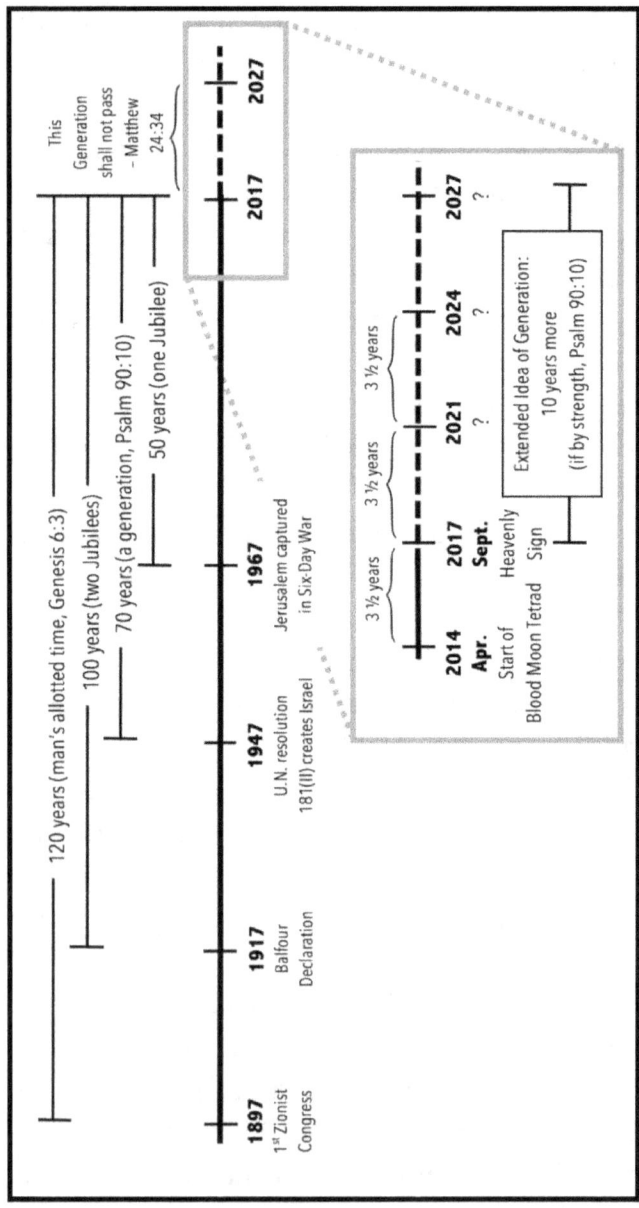

Fig. xxii: Countdown to the year 2017

2027-28 (figure xxii).

This book, as I said earlier, is not about trying to prove some final number but to inform readers that we are in a zone, standing at the very edge; perhaps even within its doors.

Whichever way it cuts, we are looking at a short period ahead.

How do we ensure our bond with Christ?

It is a personal choice we make, to be saved by grace. It is a free gift from God, to be accepted of our free will through faith, (Eph.2:8-9).

How do we accept this gift?

(Presupposing baptism, John 3:5) – *if thou shalt confess with thy mouth the Lord Jesus, and shalt believe in thine heart that God hath raised him from the dead, thou shalt be saved,* (Rom.10:9).

How do we safeguard against the evil of the last days? Stay informed, stay strong in Christ. Hold fast to his holy word and do not deny his name. *Be not afraid, neither be thou dismayed: for the LORD thy God is with thee whithersoever thou goest,* (Joshua 2:9). *Stand therefore, having your loins girt about with truth, and having on the breastplate of righteousness; And your feet shod with the preparation of the gospel of peace: Above all taking the shield of faith, wherewith we shall be able to quench all the fiery darts of the wicked, And take the helmet of salvation and the sword of the Spirit, which is the word of God,* (Eph.6:14-17).

Now the God of hope fill you with all joy and peace in believing, that ye may abound in hope through the power of the Holy Ghost, (Rom.15:13).

Blessed are they that have not seen, and yet have believed, (John 20:29).

Dear friend and fellow traveller, you have been chosen to stand in the end zone. The command, *Come out of her, my people* asks you to step out of the matrix; to awaken and to watch.

You are called to victory in Jesus Christ.

Will you stand with your saviour?

Are you ready?

About the Author

Valerie Drego holds a Ph.D. in literature and a post graduate Diploma in Business Management. She is a short story writer and poet. She received the Editor's Choice Award for Outstanding Achievement in Poetry, presented by the National Library of Poetry, Canada, 1998.

She is also a novelist and non-fiction author.

Her crime novel, *The Rhymester*, was judged a finalist in an open competition hosted by Crime Writers of Canada for the Unhanged Arthur Award, 2012.

Her non-fiction work, *End Zone*, is a study of Bible prophecy and the last days.

Her books are available on Amazon, Indigo, Barnes & Noble and through major international distribution outlets, and in consignment through her publisher In Our Words Inc., www.inourwords.ca.

www.ingramcontent.com/pod-product-compliance
Lightning Source LLC
Chambersburg PA
CBHW071604080526
44588CB00010B/1014